SAVAGE SATIRE

THE STORY OF

JONATHAN
SWIFT

SAVAGE SATIRE

THE STORY OF

JONATHAN
SWIFT

Clarissa Aykroyd

MORGAN REYNOLDS
PUBLISHING
Greensboro, North Carolina

WORLD WRITERS

Charles Dickens
Jane Austen
Ralph Ellison
Stephen King
Robert Frost
O. Henry
Roald Dahl
Jonathan Swift

Library of Congress Cataloging-in-Publication Data

Aykroyd, Clarissa.
    Savage satire : the story of Jonathan Swift / by Clarissa Aykroyd. — 1st
ed.
        p. cm.
    Includes bibliographical references and index.
    ISBN-13: 978-1-59935-027-1 (lib. bdg.)
    ISBN-10: 1-59935-027-0 (lib. bdg.)
    1. Swift, Jonathan, 1667-1745—Juvenile literature. 2. Swift, Jonathan,
1667-1745—Political and social views—Juvenile literature. 3. Authors,
Irish—18th century—Biography—Juvenile literature. 4. Satirists, Irish—
18th century—Biography—Juvenile literature. 5. Church of Ireland—Clergy—
Biography—Juvenile literature. I. Title.
    PR3726.A97 2006
    828'.509—dc22
    [B]
                                                          2006018142

Printed in the United States of America
First Edition

To my family, for their love and support

Contents

Jonathan Swift. (Courtesy of the Granger Collection.)

CHAPTER ONE

Dubliner

In 1729, poverty was a terrible problem in Ireland, a country that had been controlled by England for hundreds of years. That year a pamphlet was published that offered a simple solution for Irish poverty. The pamphlet, which was widely read in both Ireland and England, was entitled *A Modest Proposal for Preventing the Children of Poor People in Ireland from Being a Burden to their Parents or Country, and for Making Them Beneficial to the Public.*

Although the title suggested a real and practical solution to a serious problem, anyone who had read other works by the pamphlet's author might well have been wary of its contents. Jonathan Swift was a dynamic and forceful Anglo-Irishman—Irish by birth and upbringing, but from an English background. Swift was known as a man with strong political and religious convictions with a talent for writing savage, even bitter, satire. His attacks on injustice and corruption were anything but predictable.

A Modest Proposal was no exception. "I have been assured by a very knowing American of my Acquaintance in London," it stated, "that a young healthy Child, well nursed, is, at a Year old, a most delicious, nourishing, and wholesome Food; whether Stewed, Roasted, Baked, or Boiled." The proposal went on to suggest that "[t]hose who are more thrifty (as I must confess the Times require) may flay the Carcase; the Skin of which, artificially dressed will make admirable Gloves for Ladies, and Summer Boots for fine Gentlemen."

Swift's suggestion for curing Irish poverty was to eat the babies. Those readers who took *A Modest Proposal* seriously were horrified by its seemingly straightforward manner. Most readers, though, understood the point of Swift's satire. Although there were many things about Ireland and the Irish that Swift did not admire, his pamphlet did not intend to target Irish children or their poverty-stricken parents. *A Modest Proposal* was actually an attack on the rich English landowners in Ireland, who were draining the country's economy and causing great suffering for the Irish people while the English people fretted disingenuously about the poverty. "I GRANT this Food will be somewhat dear," Swift sarcastically stated, "and therefore very proper for Landlords, who, as they have already devoured most of the Parents, seem to have the best Title to the Children."

Jonathan Swift was a master of satire. He used humor

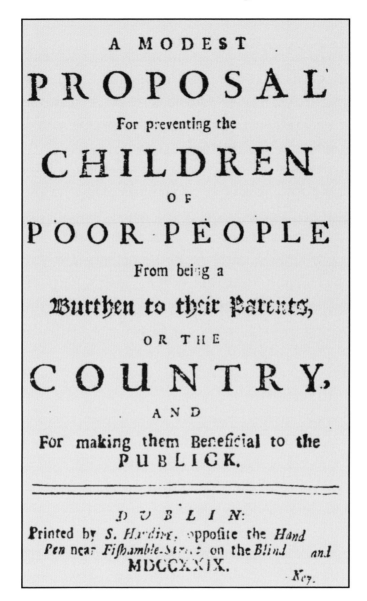

A Modest Proposal *has become, perhaps, the world's best-known satire.* (Thompson Gale)

and irony to make a point, often by saying one thing while meaning the opposite. He criticized ideas and people with whom he disagreed by mocking them and generated controversy and inflamed public opinion by using words to shape political and religious issues. Swift's books, poems, and other works remain memorable centuries later because of their power to startle and raise questions in the reader's mind.

Swift often comes across as a bitter man in his writings and also in stories about his public and private lives. Some people have called him a misanthrope—a hater of human beings. It is true that Swift used his creativity to mock and criticize his country, politics, and the human race. But his writing had a purpose: he wanted to see his words bring about a change for the better. Angry and powerful, funny and sad, Swift's works point to the capacity for good and for evil within all people—and the wish that they would improve.

Swift's most famous book, *Gulliver's Travels*, is often read as a children's fantasy, but it was written as a satire on politics and colonialism. In writing the book, he later told a friend, he hoped that it would "wonderfully mend the World." A religious man, Swift wanted to goad people into making the right choices.

Swift was born on November 30, 1667, in the gray seaside city of Dublin, Ireland. His birthplace, 7 Hoey's Court, stood close to the Liffey River, a narrow waterway that divides Dublin as it flows slowly to the sea. Nearby stood the famous Trinity College, where Swift later studied, and St. Patrick's Cathedral, which would play an important part in his religious career.

The city of Dublin had begun as one of the many small

In Swift's day Dublin was experiencing a population explosion and had already started developing suburbs. This vantage point is from Sarah's Bridge, which spans the Liffey River, about a mile from central Dublin. (British Library)

Irish settlements that sprang up along the Liffey River during the sixth century. In 837, Dubh Linn, which in the native Gaelic language means "black pool," fell under the control of Viking warriors from Norway. The Vikings were conquering Irish settlements to use as seaports. Over the next two hundred years, the Vikings and the Irish battled for control of these ports. Finally, in 1014, the forces of legendary Irish High King Brian Ború defeated the Vikings at the Battle of Clontarf, in modern-day north Dublin.

Ireland soon fell under the control of yet another foreign power. In 1170, the English king Henry II captured Dublin.

For a long time England controlled only the area immediately around Dublin, called "the Pale." It took a few hundred years before the English succeeded in extending their rule to parts of Ireland outside of this area, or "beyond the Pale." Once the English captured Ireland, they held it for centuries.

In his unfinished autobiography, *Family of Swift*, Jonathan Swift described how his English family came to live in Ireland, the land of his birth. Most of what is known about Swift's family and his early years comes from this autobiographical fragment, which he wrote toward the end of his life, but scholars still dispute its reliability. Swift was not above exaggerating for effect even when supposedly telling the factual history of his family and childhood.

Swift wrote that his grandfather, Thomas Swift, served as a vicar, or parson, for the Church of England (also referred to as the Anglican Church) in Herefordshire, England. According to Jonathan, his grandfather had many children—"ten Sons and three or four Daughters, most of which lived to be Men and Women." After the vicar died in 1658, some of his sons moved from England to Ireland.

One of these immigrants to Ireland, named Jonathan, found work in the law courts of Dublin as a clerk. He married a woman named Abigail Errick, who came from an ancient English family, according to Swift. Among her distinguished ancestors was Erick the Forester, who in 1066 had fought against the Normans during William the Conqueror's invasion of England. Abigail gave birth to a daughter and was soon pregnant again. However, her husband died months before the birth of his son and namesake, Jonathan Swift.

Despite his pride in his English ancestors, Jonathan Swift had difficulty getting along with his living relatives. He was not close to his sister and wrote that his family members were "of all mortals what I despise and hate." In his autobiography, he also passed judgment on his parent's short-lived marriage, describing it as "on both sides very indiscreet; for his wife brought her husband little or no fortune, and his death / happening so suddenly before he could make a sufficient establishment for his family" meant that young Jonathan was born into a family with little money. After the sudden death of her husband, Abigail had to depend upon her wealthy brother-in-law Godwin Swift for financial support.

Swift preferred his mother to the rest of his family, but he claimed she did not always protect him. According to *Family of Swift,* when he was an infant his nurse kidnapped him and took him to Whitehaven, England, where her relatives lived. The journey there involved a treacherous voyage by ship across the Irish Sea. The only reason given for the nurse's action was that she was "extremely fond of the infant." According to the account, in which Swift wrote about himself in the third person, Abigail took the stealing of her son quite calmly. "For when the matter was discovered," Swift explained, "His Mother sent orders by all means not to hazard a second voyage, till he could be better able to bear it."

Young Jonathan ended up staying in Whitehaven,

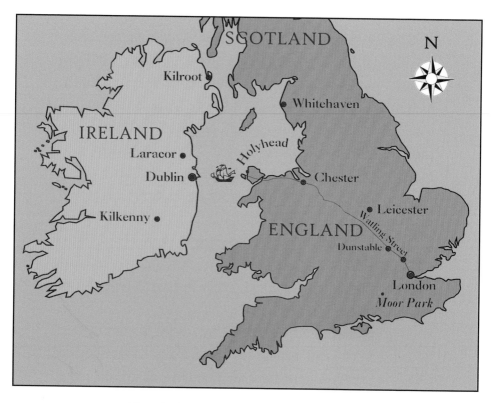

The principal locations of Jonathan Swift's life.

England, for three years. As an adult, he would fondly remember his time in the harbor town. Swift's unusual visit to England was the first of many visits that he would make to that country over the course of his life. It was during his stay in Whitehaven that Swift's fascination with the written word first began. In his autobiography, he reported that his nurse helped him with his letters and that he could read any chapter in the Bible by the age of three.

When he was around four years old, Jonathan was returned to his family. Shortly after his return, his mother left Ireland and went to live in with her family in Leicester, England. She left Jonathan and his older sister, Jane, in the care of their uncle, Godwin.

At age six, Jonathan began his schooling in Kilkenny, a stately medieval town located southeast of Dublin. He attended a boarding school called Kilkenny College. The school's doors were open only to the sons of families who were members of the Church of Ireland, the Irish branch of the Church of England. Kilkenny was considered the best school in Ireland. Students received a strict education concentrated on Latin, Greek, religion, and good morals. The curriculum included texts such as the biblical New Testament, classical writings by authors such as Cicero, and works on morality by Anglican writers.

Years later, Swift described his schooldays as a mixture of good and bad memories. "I formerly used to envy my own Happiness—when I was a Schoolboy," he recalled, as times of "delicious Holidays, the Saterday afternoon, and the charming Custards in a blind Alley; I never considered the Confinement ten hours a day, to nouns & Verbs, the Terror of the Rod, the bloddy Noses, and broken Shins."

Kilkenny's pupils did not enjoy long, lazy summer holidays. Classes ran year-round, and pupils were allowed little time off during the school week. Not only did students attend classes almost every day, they also had to participate in regular religious instruction and prayers at the cathedral.

Even as a young boy, Swift had great confidence in his intellectual abilities and writing skills. However, he would later say his talents were not fully appreciated at Kilkenny. Even though he attended a school with an excellent academic reputation, Swift would complain that his uncle had given him "the education of a dog."

Outside of school, Jonathan spent time with his cousin Thomas, who was also a student at Kilkenny. They became close friends. Jonathan loved wordplay and enjoyed using his considerable knowledge of English and Latin to create puns and double meanings. It was a gift he used throughout his career as a writer.

After finishing their schooling, many Kilkenny students began to work, often in the same professions as their fathers. Some went overseas, to England or Spain. Jonathan Swift, however, was one of the boys who continued his education. He went on to Trinity College, the major university of Dublin. He had wanted to attend a university in England, but this was beyond his family's means. Uncle Godwin had run into financial problems and another uncle, William, had assumed responsibility for the boy's university education.

Typically, Swift did not thank his relatives for their financial help. Instead, he blamed them for his eventual poor academic record at Trinity. According to Swift, "by the ill Treatment of his nearest Relations, he was so discouraged and sunk in his Spirits, that he too much neglected his Academical Studyes."

When fourteen-year-old Jonathan began studying at

Trinity, the college had been in existence for almost a century. Founded in 1592, the school was originally laid out in a single small square, or quadrangle, outside Dublin's city walls. By 1682, when Swift enrolled, the school grounds encompassed a series of quadrangles and no longer lay entirely outside the city. In the span of ninety years, both the city of Dublin and Trinity College had grown, and the area around the college had become a fashionable area for gentlemen's residences.

Despite its growth, Trinity was still a small college in 1682. It consisted of about three hundred students, in a city of about 60,000. Like Kilkenny, it was an Anglican institution, and many of its students went on to become clergymen.

During Swift's time at Trinity, two provosts, or head officials, governed the school. The first was an English bishop, Narcissus Marsh, who served from 1679 to 1683. A very religious and scholarly man, Marsh founded a great library next to St. Patrick's Cathedral that Swift would later use extensively. When Marsh left in 1683, he grumbled about the bad behavior of Trinity's students. Dealing with the boys had left him little time for his beloved books, and he later complained, "I was quickly weary of 340 young men and boys in this lewd and debauch'd town."

This dislike was apparently mutual. When Swift wrote about Marsh years later, he had nothing good to say about Trinity's former provost. Among the insults levied was the comment, "It has been affirmed that originally he was not altogether devoid of wit, till it was extruded

The Trinity Green was a popular meeting place for the upper echelons of Dublin society. Trinity College can be seen on the right, the Irish House of Lords is on the left and the old parliament building is in the middle. (British Library)

from his head to make room for other men's thoughts."

Robert Huntington succeeded Marsh as provost. He held the position until 1692. Both Marsh and Huntington were involved in the Dublin Philosophical Society, a very influential organization during Swift's years at Trinity College. A number of similar societies existed in Europe at the time, including one at Oxford University and the Royal Society in London.

Although not a member of the Dublin Philosophical Society, which was only open to more senior scholars and professors, Swift became interested in its aims and its research. The Society's members sought to develop a better understanding of science, religion, and philosophy through discussion, observation, and experimentation.

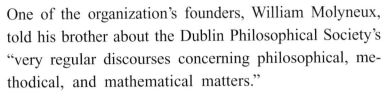

One of the organization's founders, William Molyneux, told his brother about the Dublin Philosophical Society's "very regular discourses concerning philosophical, methodical, and mathematical matters."

Just about everything was fair game for analysis by members of the Society. Members compared the effects of freezing on eggs and urine, tried to square the circle, and studied the effects of Ireland's wet and changeable weather on the barometric pressure at Trinity College. Some members pumped dogs full of water and performed other cruel experiments on animals.

In his later writings, Swift would poke fun at the kind of experimentation and research performed by the Dublin Philosophical Society. Although he had an inquiring mind, the young student felt more comfortable with—and soon turned his attention to—the study of history and literature, rather than natural science.

One of the members of the Dublin Philosophical Society was St. George Ashe, a professor of mathematics at the college and an enthusiastic experimenter. He also eventually became a provost at the college, although he held the position for only a few years. As a professor, Ashe personally tutored a small group of twenty Trinity students that included Swift. A religious man, Ashe praised mathematics as the greatest form of reasoning. Despite some differences of opinion, he and Swift became close friends.

The course of study at Trinity College included Latin, Greek, Hebrew, philosophy, mathematics, and science. Students were expected to speak to their professors and

Jonathan Swift during his time at Trinity College. (National Portrait Gallery)

to one another in Latin, even outside of class. Swift and his peers also had to master the basics of logic. They attended classes that included debates and logical reasoning on philosophical questions.

As at Kilkenny, students were expected to attend regular religious services and group prayers. Those who did not attend were supposed to pay a penny fine, but many students missed the services regularly. Thomas Wilson, one of Swift's classmates, later became a bishop, but as a student he missed chapel at least fifty times in less than a year.

Jonathan Swift was not always a well-behaved student.

Although he claimed to have "lived with great Regularity and due Observance of the Statutes," he sometimes got into trouble for such infractions as starting fights. Shortly before graduation, he was reprimanded by school officials for "neglect of duties and frequenting the town." Such behavior tarnished his record, and his academic record was not outstanding either. He received his bachelor of arts degree *speciali gratia*, or "by special grace," which meant that his record would not normally have been good enough for him to receive his BA, but the college granted him the degree anyway.

In his autobiography, Swift acknowledged his undistinguished academic record, explaining that "he was stopped of his Degree, for Dullness and Insufficiency, and at last hardly admitted in a manner little to his Credit." Still, his years at Trinity College were not a complete loss. While there, he had formed some close friendships and learned more about where his interests lay, which forms of reasoning he admired, and which ones he considered a waste of time.

After graduation, Swift continued his studies at Trinity College in pursuit of a master of arts degree. However, in 1689 the political and religious climate in Ireland became dangerous for members of the Anglican Church. The outbreak of what Swift later referred to as "the Troubles" in England and Ireland made it unsafe for him to remain in Dublin. Once again, he traveled back across the Irish Sea, to England, and to the start of his true intellectual development.

CHAPTER TWO

Moor Park

The political and religious troubles that forced Jonathan Swift to leave Ireland in 1689 had their roots in the Protestant Reformation, a cataclysmic change in Europe that had begun about 150 years earlier. For more than a thousand years the Catholic Church, centered in Rome, had been the Christian Church in Western and most of Central Europe. The Church had effectively ruled over Europe's religious, political, and cultural life. There had been centuries of conflicts between secular rulers and the Church over matters of finance and the power to appoint church officials, which the Church usually won in the end. However, the conflict and other tensions, including theological disputes and corruption inside the monolithic Church, slowly eroded the Church's authority.

During the sixteenth century, the threat to the supremacy

of the Roman Catholic Church became more open and decisive. Even monks and others within the Church began to question its doctrines and to attack it for corruption. The most important of these rebellious monks was a German named Martin Luther, who was a professor at a university in Wittenberg, in the German state of Saxony. In 1517, Luther nailed a letter outlining his complaints against the Catholic Church to the door of the cathedral in Wittenberg, Germany. This was a common way to communicate in the city.

Luther's criticisms were both doctrinal and political. As he continued to criticize the Church, he gained supporters.

Martin Luther, as portrayed by Lucas Cranach the Elder, in 1529. Cranach, a personal friend, attended Luther's wedding to Katharina von Bora, an ex-nun. (Galleria degli Uffizi)

The time was ripe for a serious break with the Church's leadership in faraway Rome.

Luther and others wanted to change the Church's teachings regarding the proper role the Church should play in an individual believer's relationship with the deity. The idea that human beings can come to God without the mediation of the Church was a direct blow to papal tradition and power. There were thousands ready to hear Luther's message, and he is credited with starting the Protestant Reformation. Called Protestants because they protested against the corruption and doctrine of the Catholic Church, they eventually established a separate Christian faith. Eventually, Protestant groups splintered into dozens, then hundreds, of smaller denominations. The official German form of Protestantism became known as Lutheranism.

The Reformation also gave ambitious secular rulers, long impatient with Church interference in what they considered to be their affairs, an opportunity to break from the Church. Many of the rulers of the small German states, particularly in the north, seized on the opportunity, as did most of the Scandinavian kings. At first, the rulers of England and Scotland resisted the Reformation. King Henry VIII of England (1491–1547) initially condemned Luther's ideas. In 1521, Pope Leo X, in his capacity as supreme head of the Roman Catholic Church, honored the English king by naming him the "Defender of the Faith." But soon Henry VIII bristled at the power the pope held over his political and personal life.

By the late 1520s, Henry wanted to end his marriage to

Henry VIII, a Protestant by convenience, broke with the pope in order to marry and then divorce, kill, or drive to the grave a string of five women. His widow (the sixth wife) was merely a nursemaid to the much older, gangrenous, and obese king. (Museo Thyssen-Bornemisza, Madrid)

Catherine of Aragon, who had not given him a living son. He was smitten by a woman at his court, Anne Boleyn, and was eager to have his marriage to Catherine annulled. But he needed the pope's permission, which was not forthcoming. Queen Catherine's nephew was Charles V, the powerful Holy Roman Emperor, whose troops had only recently sacked Rome because of a dispute. The pope, who could not afford to offend the emperor again, denied Henry's request.

An enraged Henry then rejected the Catholic Church's authority. In 1533, an English court granted Henry VIII a divorce so that he could marry Anne Boleyn. The following year, the English parliament passed the Act of Supremacy, which designated the king as the political and religious head of the English people. A new church was born—the Anglican Church, or Church of England.

At first, Henry did not want to reject Catholicism completely, but during the 1530s the Anglican Church moved away from the teachings and doctrines of Catholicism and closer to those of Protestantism. At the same time, other Protestant denominations were being established in England. Eventually the politically powerful came to view the Catholic Church as a threat to England and to the English throne.

While the English accepted Protestantism as their religious faith, most Irish people remained Roman Catholic. Only a minority of the population of Ireland was non-Catholic, and most of them were English or of English descent. In Ireland, people referred to the Anglican Church as the Church of Ireland, and the native Irish often viewed it as a symbol of English oppression.

During the rule of the English king Charles I, in the 1630s and 1640s, differences in religion and politics led to several uprisings in Scotland and Ireland. Charles I was suspected of being a secret Catholic. He also held to the doctrine called the divine right of kings—that a monarch's authority comes directly from God and should therefore be obeyed without question. His clumsy attempts to impose religious reforms in both Scotland, where Presbyterianism, a form of Protestantism, had taken hold, and in Ireland, created many enemies. As head of the Church of England, a role held by all English monarchs since its establishment, Charles was suspected of trying to introduce Roman Catholic policies into the English church.

The tensions grew until, in 1642, a civil war broke out. Charles's supporters, known as Royalists, supported the king's beliefs and policies. The Royalists were opposed by supporters of the English parliament—a governmental body of noblemen, clergymen, and knights who had rejected the sovereign's claim of absolute power and his support for Catholics. In England, fighting between the Royalists and parliamentary forces ended in 1649, when Charles I was executed.

The commander of the parliamentary forces, Oliver Cromwell, took charge after the death of Charles. He ruled as Lord Protector over England, Ireland, and Scotland in a newly established government called the Commonwealth of England. From 1649 to 1652, Cromwell savagely battled Royalist forces based in Ireland, from the city of Dublin in the east to the city of Galway in the west. Cromwell's forces killed thousands of Irish. The continuing violence in Ireland fueled further hatred between the Roman Catholic Irish and the Protestant English.

After Oliver Cromwell died in 1658, his government collapsed. In 1660, the son of King Charles I was crowned king of England as Charles II. Because the monarchy was restored with his coronation, Charles II's reign, which lasted twenty-five years, is often referred to as the Restoration. Like his father, Charles II sympathized with the Catholics, although he did not convert to Catholicism until just before his death in 1685.

After the death of Charles II, his younger brother, who had converted to Catholicism, succeeded him. As king of England, James II gave greater rights to Catholics, encouraged the establishment of Catholic schools, and permitted Catholics to attend the great English universities of Oxford and Cambridge.

Most English nobles feared that James II planned to try to return England to the religious faith that had been rejected under Henry VIII and set off yet another bloody conflict. In 1688, members of the English nobility invited the king's Protestant son-in-law, the Dutch prince William of Orange, to invade England and seize the crown. William's wife, Mary, was one of James II's daughters. She had been born and raised as a Protestant and remained a devout member of the faith, despite her father's conversion to Catholicism.

In November 1688, William of Orange landed in England in what came to be known as the Glorious Revolution. James II fled to Catholic France, and the following year the members of parliament appointed King William III and Queen Mary II as rulers of the kingdoms of England and Ireland. Parliament, however, ensured that the rulers' powers were not absolute.

England's political and religious turmoil engulfed Ireland once again when, in an effort to regain the throne, James II landed on the island in April 1689. The Irish parliament supported his claim to the throne, as did some prominent Catholics, including officials at Trinity College. Fearful for their safety, many Protestant families in Ireland

John Turner portrays the miraculous crossing of William and Mary. As the story goes, a "Protestant wind" blew the royal couple straight to England while it simultaneously kept the British fleet from setting sail. The crossing, however providential, was far from easy for the 15,000 men and 4,000 horses riding on the storm-tossed sea. (Courtesy of Art Resource.)

fled to England. By this time, Jonathan Swift had already returned to his ancestral land.

Upon arriving in England, Swift stayed with his mother in Leicester. A few months later, he went to Moor Park, the home of Sir William Temple, in Surrey. Swift found employment there, he later explained, because Sir William Temple's father "had been a great Friend to the Family." Temple's father had been the head of the Irish Bar, an official association of lawyers, and Jonathan's father had worked under him.

Jonathan applied for the job, according to his cousin Deane Swift, at his mother's suggestion. According to Deane, Abigail considered William Temple to be "both a

great and a wise man." Temple himself said of his patron-
age of Swift: "[H]is whole family having been long
known to mee obliged mee . . . to take care of Him." The
early relationship between the two men was based on a
long association between their families. When Swift
joined Temple's household, he became like another
member of the family.

Sir William Temple's roots were in Ireland. His grandfather had been a provost at Trinity College, and his father

A man of wide experience and talent, Sir William Temple undoubtedly influenced Swift's understanding of the world. (British Museum)

was Irish by birth. Temple himself was English, but he was as much a citizen of the world as it was possible to be in the seventeenth century. He had spent years working for the English government, mostly as a diplomat. One of his greatest achievements as a statesman was negotiating the Triple Alliance of 1668, an agreement involving England, the Netherlands, and Sweden that bound them together against the growing power of France.

The Triple Alliance did not last, but Temple had achieved success in other political negotiations, particularly the arranged marriage between William of Orange and James II's daughter Mary before they came to the throne. After retiring from politics, Temple maintained contact with King William, who would consult the elder statesman for advice.

A well-educated man, Temple loved art, literature, and beautiful things. He had designed the carefully laid-out gardens of Moor Park, which featured a canal, fruit trees, and woods.

Swift worked for Temple as his secretary and personal assistant. In those early days, the retired diplomat had an enormous influence on Swift, who came to admire his employer as "a man of virtue." However, Swift's stay at Moor Park lasted only one year. In May 1690, Temple sent the young man back to Ireland—not because he did not like his employee, but because he wanted to help advance Swift's professional career. Temple had asked the king's secretary of state to find Swift a position in Ireland, perhaps at Trinity College.

Swift returned to Ireland at a bad time. Since arriving in the country the previous year, James II had been gathering Catholic forces around him in preparation to fight for the English crown against King William. In July 1690, he was defeated at the Battle of the Boyne, which was fought among the green fields and rolling hills by the Boyne River, near Dublin. Ireland was now facing a violent and uncertain future, and the country held no employment prospects for Swift.

In his autobiography, however, Swift seems less concerned with the volatile political situation in his native land than with the effects of its climate on his health. Ireland was even colder and wetter than England, he noted. Before his trip Swift had begun to suffer from a health problem that he described as "giddiness." Today, physicians refer to this sickness as Menière's disease, or labyrinthine vertigo. The illness affects the inner ear, causing episodes of hearing loss, dizziness, tinnitus, and pain.

Swift had traveled to Ireland in hope not only of finding a job, but also of getting better. As he explained in his autobiography, "[H]e returned to Ireld by advice of Physicians, who weakly imagined that his native air might be of some use to recover his Health. But growing worse, he soon went back to Sir Wm Temple." The disease would trouble him for the rest of his life.

William III's forces had completed the conquest of Ireland by the time Swift returned to Moor Park in 1691. He would remain there for the next three years. During this time, he completed his master of arts degree at Hart Hall, which

Moor Park was Swift's home for the larger part of the years between 1689 and 1695.

is part of the University of Oxford. However, he spent most of his time with Temple and his household. During this critical period Swift started to write seriously, and he met a young girl named Esther Johnson, whom he called Stella. His friendship with Stella would last for most of his life.

Stella was the daughter of one of Temple's house-keepers. When she and Swift first met, she was a small, sickly girl, only eight years old, while he was twenty-two. Temple treated the little girl like a daughter, and Swift soon grew fond of her. "I . . . had some share in her education, by directing what books she should read, and perpetually instructing her in the principles of honour and virtue," he later said.

At the same time that he was contributing to Stella's education, Swift was also polishing his writing skills. After retiring from politics, William Temple had become a prolific writer. As Temple's secretary and assistant, Swift transcribed many of his patron's works, which included political essays, memoirs, and poetry. He also translated into English works that Temple had originally written in French.

While copying out Temple's writings, Swift started to see how he could express his own strong ideas and feelings. Over the next few years, he wrote several odes—an elevated style of poetry—on serious subjects such as war and philosophy. He also wrote lighter verses, such as a poem to celebrate Temple's recovery after an illness. These early writings show the influence of his patron. Although Swift would write many poems during his life, the satirical style that was to become his hallmark did not appear until later.

As he struggled to find the words to express his thoughts, Swift experienced the trials that all writers endure. He often grew frustrated and unhappy with the quality of his work, and burned most of it as trash. Shortly after returning to Moor Park, he complained, "[I]n these seven weeks I have been here, I have writt, & burnt and writt again, upon almost all manner of subjects, more perhaps that any man in England."

The household at Moor Park was a close-knit one. In addition to Temple, Swift, and Stella, its members included Temple's wife, Dorothy Osborne, and his sister, Lady Giffard. Everyone, including Swift, was extremely fond of Temple. In fact, one of the first poems that Swift wrote honored his patron. In "Ode to the Honourable Sir William Temple," Swift celebrated the statesman's virtues with reverential lines such as "Shall I believe a spirit so divine / Was cast in the same mould with mine?"

Temple, in turn, gave Swift many important privileges. On one occasion, Swift was asked to act as Temple's representative before King William. But when the young man made his presentation, the king refused him. "This was the first time that Mr Swift had ever any converse with Courts," Swift reported later in his autobiography, "and he told his friends it was the first incident that helped to cure him of vanity."

Although Swift held a privileged position in Temple's household, the relationship between the two men was sometimes strained. Swift took offense whenever his patron seemed to be in a bad mood, or showed some coldness toward him. Swift also began to believe that Temple was interested only in using him as a talented and competent secretary, rather than helping him advance in his chosen profession. Like many other graduates of Trinity College, Swift had decided that a career in the Anglican Church best suited his abilities. He hoped—in fact, he expected—that Temple would use his influence to find him an important position in the Church of England. But as the years passed, he started to wonder whether Temple would help him secure such a position. "[T]ho' he promises me the certainty of it, yet [he] is less forward than I could wish, because I suppose he believes I shall leave him, and upon some accounts, he thinks me a little necessary to him," he complained in a letter to his uncle, William Swift.

Up until this time, Swift had not shown any interest in going back to live in Ireland. England, and especially Moor Park, felt like his real home. He wanted to become a priest in the Anglican Church, and he also wanted to stay in England. But Temple did not seem to be helping him in that direction. Instead, he urged the young man to be patient. Finally, in 1694, Swift resolved that he would go back to Ireland, and take holy orders with the Anglican Church there.

By the time Swift left Moor Park, he was no longer on good terms with his employer. In a letter to his cousin Deane Swift, Jonathan wrote of Temple that "He was extream angry I left Him, and yet would not oblige Himself any further than upon my good Behaviour, nor would promise any thing firmly to Me at all, so that every Body judged I did best to leave Him."

Upon his return to Ireland, Swift prepared to be ordained as a priest. However, he soon learned that he could not break off all contact with Temple. Since several years had passed since Swift had completed his degree at Trinity College, the bishops who had agreed to ordain him—including the hated Narcissus Marsh—wanted a written testimonial of his good character. A very humble letter from Swift to Temple requesting the recommendation was the result:

> That I might not continue by any means the many
> Troubles I [have] given You; I have all this while

avoyded one, which I fear proves necessary at last. [. . .] my Lord ArchBishop of Dublin [Narcissus Marsh] . . . expected I should have a Certificate from Your Honor, of my Conduct in your Family. The Sense I am in, how low I am fallen in Your Honor's Thoughts, has denied Me Assurance enough to beg this Favor till I find it impossible to avoyd.

Temple was kind enough to send a quick and courteous reply, and there was no further delay. Swift was ordained in January 1695, in Dublin's Christ Church Cathedral, very close to its sister cathedral, St. Patrick's. His birthplace of Ireland was strengthening its hold on him.

CHAPTER THREE

"For the Universal Improvement of Mankind"

Although ordained as a priest in the city of his birth, Jonathan Swift did not receive a church assignment in Dublin. Instead, he was awarded a modest salary of about one hundred British pounds a year and sent to the far north of Ireland, as vicar to the parish of Kilroot. Located near the North Channel, close to the towns of Belfast and Carrickfergus, Kilroot was surrounded by wild and beautiful scenery, with views stretching down to the sea.

Despite its beauty, Kilroot was a lonely and frustrating place for an ambitious man like Swift, who was constantly looking for intellectual stimulation. The parish had a small church, which lay in ruins. Although the nearby churches of Templecorran and Ballynure were usable, their congregations were small. Many of the Anglican churches in the area were ruined or in bad shape. Worse, just before Swift's appointment to Kilroot, some of the clergymen in the area had been accused of immoral behavior and stealing Church of Ireland funds.

For Swift, one of the biggest disadvantages of his appointment to Kilroot was the power of Presbyterianism

The counties of Ireland. Swift spent most of his time in Antrim, Kilkenny, and Dublin Counties.

in the area. Although a Protestant faith, Presbyterianism was considered a Nonconformist sect because the Presbyterian Church did not follow the beliefs and rules of the Anglican Church. A local man, Richard Dobbs, who became one of Swift's friends, explained in a letter to Swift that most of the people living in the area were from Scotland and were Nonconformists. "[T]he inhabitants (except my family and some half a dozen that live under me) [are] all Presbyterians and Scotch," he explained. "[There is] not one natural Irish in the parish, nor papist."

The town of Belfast had an especially large number of Presbyterians. Because there were so many Presbyterians

Belfast grew exponentially in Swift's time. It had already become an industrial center. A mill can be seen to the left, with Belfast in the background. (British Library)

and other Nonconformists in the north of Ireland, the English government did not try to discourage or suppress them, because of the risk of inciting rebellion. Swift disliked all Nonconformists. He was irritated that local Presbyterian meetings drew many worshipers, while his own church meetings attracted only small numbers of parishioners.

Despite the many problems that Swift faced as vicar of the parish, and the general lack of congenial company, he did manage to make some friends during his time in Kilroot. He spent time with Richard Dobbs, who was a member of the church at Templecorran, in his home of Castle Dobbs. The extensive library there was a pleasant diversion for the young clergyman. Swift also liked and admired Henry Clements, the mayor of Carrickfergus, and John Winder, the vicar of Carnmoney. Already known to be a critical man, Swift once gave Winder an exceptional compliment in a letter, when he admitted to "having never entertained one single ill thought of You in my life."

During the year Jonathan Swift spent at Kilroot, a young woman came into his life. Jane Waring was from Waringstown, a village named after her family. The daughter of an archdeacon who had died a few years before Swift arrived at Kilroot, Jane was seven years younger than Swift, and was in poor health. Swift had known Jane's brother and cousins at Trinity College. He referred to the young woman as Varina, a Latin nickname based on her family name.

Little is known about the relationship between the two, except for what survives in a few letters that they exchanged. Although Swift asked Jane to marry him, her letters indicate that she was uncertain about her feelings toward him, or whether it would be wise to marry him. He, in turn, urged her to make up her mind. "[H]ow far you will stretch the point of your unreasonable scruples to keep me here, will depend upon the strength of the love you pretend for me," he implored.

Swift wrote like a man in love. He insisted that her acceptance of his proposal would restore her health, and wondered what force kept her from accepting him. "Varina's life is daily wasting," he said, "and though one just and honourable action would furnish health to her, and un-speakable happiness to us both, yet some power that repines at human felicity has that influence to hold her continually doating on her cruelty, and me upon the cause of it." He concluded his letter dramatically, stating, "Only remember, that if you still refuse to be mine, you will quickly lose, for ever lose, him that is resolved to die as he has lived, all yours, Jon. Swift."

This piece of correspondence was Swift's final effort to get Jane to marry him. He would soon leave Ireland. Disappointed by his experiences in Kilroot, he had no desire to stay any longer.

Swift had another incentive to return to England. As he loftily informed Jane Waring, "I am once more offered the advantage to have the same acquaintance with greatness that I formerly enjoyed, and with better prospect of inter-est." He was referring to his restored relationship with Sir William Temple. After Jonathan's departure for Ireland, his cousin Thomas Swift had replaced him as secretary, but had not stayed. Temple suggested to Jonathan that if he returned to the position, he might have an opportunity to acquire a position within the Church in England.

Swift did not believe he was accomplishing much in the lonely and isolated northern corner of his native land. With the prospect of a renewed friendship with Temple, and a return to his old home of Moor Park, the decision to leave Ireland came easily. In his autobiography, he simply stated that after "growing weary [of Kilroot] in a few months, he returned to England."

In 1696, Swift left Ireland without Jane Waring. She had refused his marriage proposal, although her rejection did not bring about the end of their correspondence. Back in Moor Park, he waited for more than a year before officially resigning from his position in Kilroot, even though his decision to relinquish the post had been made before he actually left Ireland. However, his hopes for obtaining an important church position in England came to nothing. Temple advised Swift to try to renew his position at Kilroot, but the young clergyman was happy to give up the lonely Irish parish and continue for a few more years at Moor Park.

Swift again worked mainly as a literary assistant to Temple. The aging diplomat was in poor health, and needed help in preparing his many writings for publication. Swift spent much of his time transcribing and translating Temple's letters, memoirs, essays, and poetry.

Swift also worked on his own literary efforts. It was during these years at Moor Park that he wrote his first major works of satire. Although satire had previously been used in plays and poetry, Swift was the first to make use of this literary technique in prose writing. Satire usually makes use of language devices such as irony (in which the real meaning is concealed or contradicted), ridicule (mockery), and parody (imitation of a style or work). Satiric writings generally criticize faults—in individuals, groups, or society in general—in order to bring about change or improvement.

Scholars do not know for certain when Swift began writing the satirical piece *A Tale of a Tub*, which he ambitiously subtitled *Written for the Universal Improvement of Mankind.* It is a long, complicated essay in which Swift uses irony and parody to attack the wrongs and abuses that he saw in his society, specifically in religion, literature, and education.

A Tale of a Tub begins like a fairy tale: "Once upon a Time, there was a Man who had Three Sons by one Wife, and all at a Birth, neither could the Mid-Wife tell certainly which was the Eldest." Each of the brothers—Martin, Peter, and Jack—is given a coat by his father. When the father dies, the brothers go out into the world. However, each one chooses to use his coat differently. Their choices show the direction they will take with their lives. Although their father left specific instructions in his will about how the coats were to be used, Jack and Peter go against these instructions. Eventually, they twist their father's wishes to suit their own purposes.

Swift's story is an allegory, a form of literature in which symbolic fictional figures are used to present a deeper level

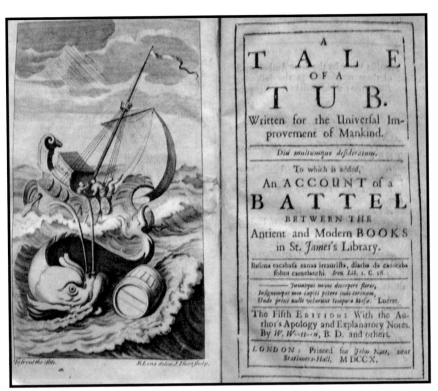

A
T A L E
OF A
T U B.
Written for the Univerfal Im-
provement of Mankind.

Diu multumque defideratum.

To which is added,

An ACCOUNT of a
B A T T E L
BETWEEN THE
Antient and Modern BOOKS
in St. James's Library.

Bafima eacabafa eanaa irraurifta, diarba da caaotaba
fobor camnlanthi. *Iren. Lib. i. C. 18.*

————— *Juvatque novos decerpere flores,
Infignemque meo capiti petere inde coronam,
Unde prius nulli velarunt tempora Mufæ.* Lucret.

The Fifth EDITION: With the Author's Apology and Explanatory Notes.
By W. W--tt--n, B. D. and others.

LONDON, Printed for John Nutt, near
Stationers-Hall, MDCCX.

This image depicting Swift's most complex satire, A Tale of a Tub, *uses a whale to represent Thomas Hobbes's controversial book the* Leviathan. *The tub is a pun referencing the pulpit and the names of the three brothers derive from church founders, Martin Luther, Saint Peter, and John Calvin.* (Purdue University, Indiana)

of meaning. In this case, the three brothers symbolize three different Christian churches: the Anglican Church (Martin), the Roman Catholic Church (Peter), and Calvinism (Jack), which is a Nonconformist sect. The father represents God, and his written will symbolizes the Bible, left for Christians to follow.

To make the allegory clear to his readers, Swift added many footnotes to the text. For example, he described Jack as "a Person that feared no Colours, but mortally hated all, and upon that Account, bore a cruel Aversion to Painters." The accompanying footnote read, "They [Calvinists] quarrel at the most Innocent Decency and Ornament, and defaced the Statues and Paintings on all the Churches in England." Martin, on the other hand, carefully strips away all the unnecessary and offensive ornamentation on his coat, "resolving in no Case whatsoever, that the Substance of the Stuff should suffer Injury; which he thought the best Method for serving the true Intent and Meaning of his Father's Will." *A Tale of a Tub* revealed Swift's strong feelings about religion and his belief in the superiority of the Anglican Church.

While *A Tale of a Tub* follows a basic storyline, it also contains several "digressions" from the main plot. These digressions cover a wide range of subjects, including vanity and pride, the desire for fame, and literary criticism. For example, Swift comments wryly on "a True Critick; . . . He is a Discoverer and Collector of Writers Faults." Swift also attacks the state of modern scholarship and writing, humorously noting, "I am now trying an Experiment very frequent among Modern Authors; which is, to write upon Nothing."

While at Moor Park, Swift also wrote *The Battle of the Books*. The piece is a playful satire on the debate in literary circles about whether ancient writers are better than modern ones. In the story, the books of St. James's Library, which are divided into the Ancients (wisdom of the past) and the Moderns (scholarship of the present), are at war. They plan their military tactics and fight a pitched battle. Swift generally sides with the Ancients, and defends the interests of his patron, Sir William Temple, who believed that ancient literature was superior to anything that modern writers and critics were producing.

In the preface to *The Battle of the Books,* Swift explained his use of satire, defining it as "a sort of Glass [mirror], wherein Beholders do generally discover every body's Face but their Own; which is the chief Reason for that kind Reception it meets in the World, and that so very few are offended by it." In other words, most readers of satire thoroughly enjoy it because they do not see themselves as its target. Although Swift completed both *The Battle of the Books* and *A Tale of a Tub* while living at Moor Park, he did not publish them until several years later.

At Moor Park, Swift continued to develop his relationship with Stella, whom he had first befriended when she was a young girl. Now a teenager, Stella helped Swift with his work transcribing Temple's writings. At the same time, Swift helped her improve her reading and writing. He also continued to write to Jane Waring.

In January 1699, Sir William Temple died, and Swift was faced with having to make his own way in the world. The young man was somewhat insincere at the death of his patron. In private conversation, he spoke critically about Temple for not doing more to advance his career and recognize his talents. But in public, Swift wrote admiringly of Temple, calling him "a person of the greatest wisdom, justice, liberality, politeness, eloquence, of his age and nation . . . having been universally esteemed the most accomplished writer of his time."

In his will, Temple left Swift one hundred pounds and also made him his literary executor, giving him the responsibility of putting his writings in order and seeing that they

Stella, possibly towards the end of her stay at Moor Park. (National Gallery of Ireland)

were published. Stella received a richer legacy of £250 and some land in Ireland. In addition to preparing Temple's writings for publication, Swift also made funeral arrangements—purchasing mourning clothes for the household and paying the fee for Temple's burial at Westminster Abbey, in London.

The period following Temple's death was an uncertain time. At some point in 1699, as he tried to envision his future, Swift wrote an ironic list of resolutions entitled "When I come to be old." Included on the list were the following intentions: "Not to marry a young Woman,"

"Not to keep young Company unless they realy desire it," and "Not to be too free of advise nor trouble any but those that desire it." However, he revealed that the resolutions were made lightly, by adding a conditional rule at the list's end: it stated the goal "Not to sett up for observing all these Rules, for fear I should observe none."

After Temple's death, Swift tried to use his patron's popularity with England's powerful men to obtain an appointment for himself within the Church of England. He asked King William for a prebend (a minor clerical position) at Canterbury or Westminster Cathedral. Apparently, the king had promised Temple that Swift would receive such a favor. However, the only position that became available was that of personal priest and secretary to the Earl of Berkeley, who was going to Dublin as a lord justice of Ireland.

An appointment in Ireland was not what Swift had hoped for. After leaving Kilroot and officially giving up the parish, it seemed unlikely he would ever live in Ireland again. Still, he decided to take the appointment with the Earl of Berkeley, and joined his traveling party in August 1699.

However, much to Swift's disgust, soon after arriving in Dublin he lost his position with the earl to another man. Swift explained that "another Person had so far insinuated himself into the Earls favor, by telling him, that the Post of Secretary was not proper for a Clergyman, nor would be of any advantage to one who aimed onely at Church-preferments, that his Lordship after a poor Apology gave that Office to the other."

Swift blamed the same man, Arthur Bushe, for preventing him from receiving the position of dean of Derry, a town near his old parish of Kilroot. According to Swift, the Earl of Berkeley had the power to grant the deanery to him, but instead gave it to someone else. When Swift complained, he received a weak explanation. "The Excuse pretended was his being too young, although he were then 30 years old," Swift wrote indignantly in his autobiography. Swift was bitter about his misfortunes. He had been denied the important position he believed he deserved in England, then brought back to a country where he did not really want to live and cast adrift.

Swift's luck changed when he received an appointment as vicar for the parish of Laracor. The parish was not far from Dublin, located near the village of Trim and the site of the Battle of the Boyne. Swift was also placed in charge of the parishes of Rathbeggan and Agher. His new position paid a living of about £230 a year, which was a very good income for a clergyman in Ireland at that time. Although angry about not obtaining a more prestigious position, Swift was to find much happiness at Laracor. In addition to his parishes, he soon assumed a prebend at St. Patrick's Cathedral, in Dublin. Although the Prebend of Dunlavin was a minor clerical position, it was in one of Ireland's most important and powerful cathedrals.

In 1700, just when Swift was about to establish himself at Laracor, he received a surprising offer. Jane Waring, who had turned down his marriage proposal a few years earlier, wrote to him again. She told him that she still wanted to keep the possibility of a relationship between them open. Swift's response indicated that he was unimpressed by the suggestion. When Jane Waring had refused the young clergyman before, she had mentioned her poor health and Swift's lack of a good income as two of her reasons. In his letter, Swift turned these points back on the woman whom he had once claimed to love deeply. "The dismal account you say I have given you of my livings, I can assure you to be a true one," he wrote, "and since it is a dismal one even in your own opinion, you can best draw consequences from it."

Swift then asked Waring an aggressive series of questions, clearly outlining his intellectual and emotional requirements in a wife:

> Will you be ready to engage in those methods I shall direct for the improvement of your mind, so as to make us entertaining company for each other, without being miserable when we are neither visiting or visited. Can you bend your love and esteem and indifference to others the same way as I do mine? . . . Have you so much good nature as to endeavour by soft words to smooth any rugged humour, occasioned by the cross accidents of life?

In conclusion, Swift scolded the woman who had rejected him. "I singled you out at first from the rest of women, and I expect not to be used like a common lover," he asserted. If Swift's harsh letter was designed to end the possibility of marriage, it worked. Swift and Jane Waring did not exchange any more letters on the subject of marriage. Jane never married.

In 1701, Swift divided his time between his clerical duties in Ireland and editorial work in London, where he prepared Temple's works for publication. He was also publishing his own work, including the political pamphlet *A Discourse of the Contests and Dissensions Between the Nobles and the*

The House of Commons as it looked in Swift's day. The members of this house are democratically elected while those of the upper house, the House of Lords, serve by government appointment. (Department for Environment, Food, and Rural Affairs, England)

This highly detailed drawing of London in 1750 gives the impression of a busy, bustling metropolis. It could have functioned as a map since all the major elements are numbered and labeled.

Commons in Athens and Rome. The pamphlet discussed the power struggle going on at the time between the two major legislative bodies of the English parliament: the House of Lords and the House of Commons. In the pamphlet, Swift argued that the House of Commons had too much power. He warned that if the power was not equally shared, the government would fail, just as it had in ancient Athens and Rome.

While in London, Swift visited his "family" from Moor Park, Stella Johnson and her companion Rebecca Dingley. Although he had rejected Jane Waring, Swift was not totally opposed to the idea of some female company in his life. By the fall of 1701, Stella and Rebecca had agreed to return to Ireland with Swift, planning to live in Dublin. Swift denied that there was any romantic connection between him and Stella, although many people wondered about their relationship. According to Swift, the two young women believed that they would have more financial security if they accepted his invitation because Stella now owned land in Ireland, and living expenses there were lower than in England.

Swift also enjoyed his journeys to England because of his growing interest in its politics. In 1701, there were two major political parties: the Whigs and the Tories. The Whigs wanted a government in which the powers of the king and the powers of Parliament balanced each other, thus limiting the king's power. The Whig Party also believed that a monarch's right to rule should be based on whether or not he ruled justly, and whether or not he was accepted by the nation. Accordingly, the party had supported the overthrow of James II in 1688. The Tories, on the other hand, believed that the king's right to rule was almost absolute, and that he represented God's will. Unlike the Whigs, they were strong supporters of the Church of England.

At the turn of the eighteenth century, participants in English politics did not have to be completely committed to one party or another. It was quite possible to be a Whig in most ways, but to also have some Tory sympathies. Eventually, though, most people who were politically involved ended up choosing one side and rejecting the other. As Swift gained attention for his forceful political and religious commentary, people began asking questions about the nature of his political allegiance. It was time for him to start asking those questions of himself.

CHAPTER FOUR

Whigs, Tories, and Ladies

During the first few years of the 1700s, Swift traveled frequently between Ireland and England. When in Ireland, he visited Dublin, where he moved in social circles as a popular and entertaining guest. When Stella Johnson and Rebecca Dingley moved to the country, Swift introduced them into Dublin society. Although it was Stella who was his friend, Swift met with her only in the presence of a third person, usually Rebecca Dingley, so as to avoid any hint of scandal. Nevertheless, the close friendship between the clergyman in his mid-thirties and the pretty young woman in her early twenties did inspire some gossip.

Swift's responsibilities in Ireland kept him busy. In 1702, his alma mater, Trinity College, granted him the degree of doctor of divinity, an appropriate qualification for someone with his position in the church. Thereafter, he was referred to as Dr. Swift, or simply "the Doctor." In addition to his clerical duties, Swift worked to restore the ruined local church and planted willow trees in his garden. When the new archbishop of Dublin, William King, arrived in the city, the young vicar of Laracor made efforts to establish good relations with him.

However, Swift's interest in the politics of England continued to draw him to London, where he spent longer and longer periods of time. In November 1703, he arrived in the city to attend the meeting of the English parliament, and remained there for the next six months. In a letter written to his friend William Tisdall in Ireland, Swift explained that he felt more English than Irish: "Then for the Irish legs you reproach me with, I defy you; I had one indeed when I left your island, but that which made it Irish is spent and evaporate, and I look upon myself now as upon a new foot." Later in the letter, he mocked the land of his birth by asking "[W]ho that hath a spirit would write in such a scene as Ireland?"

Swift preferred England, and he was becoming more involved in its political issues. Although he had published *A Discourse of the Contests and Dissensions between the Nobles and the Commons in Athens and Rome* anonymously in 1701, he now revealed himself as the author to some Whig government officials who were coming under attack by the Tories. At this time, Swift was essentially a Whig supporter. He agreed with the overthrow of James II in 1688, and with limitations on a king's power in general. However, because of his strong religious beliefs, Swift could not fully support the Whigs. The Whig Party believed that non-Anglican Protestants should be given more rights. Swift opposed all non-Anglican Protestant churches.

Because he could not fully support the political and religious ideals of either the Whigs or the Tories, Swift did not identify fully with either party. Looking back on this time of indecision, Swift later admitted, "I found myself much inclined to be what they called a Whig in politics. . . . But as to religion, I confessed myself to be an High-churchman, and that I did not conceive how anyone, who wore the habit of a clergyman, could be otherwise."

After the death of King William III in 1702, James II's daughter Anne ascended to the English throne. Although the new queen often sympathized with Tories, in 1703 the Tories tried to pass a new law through Parliament that would allow only Anglicans to hold political office. In this case, Queen Anne did not side with the Tories. Because she did not support the bill, it did not pass.

A strong proponent of the Anglican Church, Swift was undecided on the issue. In discussing the proposed law in a letter to his friend Tisdall, he admitted to being confused. "I am much at a loss, though I was mightily urged by some great people to publish my opinion. I cannot but think (if mens highest assurances are to be believed) that several, who were against this bill, do love the Church, and do hate or despise Presbytery," he wrote. "I know not what to think, and therefore shall think no more."

In 1704, Swift published *Tale of a Tub* and *Battle of the Books,* the pieces he had written while living at Moor Park.

Queen Anne became the first monarch of Great Britain when Scotland and England united as one kingdom under her rule in 1707. She was the last of the Stuarts to reign since neither she nor her sister Mary II had a child survive to adulthood. (Courtesy of the Granger Collection.)

The works were published anonymously, he later said, so that they could speak for themselves. In *A Tale of a Tub,* he included a dedication to John Somers, a prominent Whig politician. Swift thought that a Whig dedication in a book that praised the Anglican Church would show his support for both the Whigs and the Tories. However, the dedication and the strong satire, which appeared to ridicule Anglican doctrines and beliefs, led many people to think that the book's creator was actually attacking the Anglican Church. Later, when it was revealed that Swift had written the work, many people questioned his religious beliefs.

As he became even more immersed in the intellectual life of England, Swift continued trying to obtain a position within the Church of England. His attempts to obtain a position proved futile, though, and he soon realized that he had to return to his duties at Laracor and St. Patrick's Cathedral. There were other reasons to return to Ireland as well: Stella Johnson and Rebecca Dingley, whom Swift referred to as "the ladies," were also on his mind.

In April of 1704, Swift learned that his friend and frequent correspondent William Tisdall had a romantic interest in Stella. Tisdall had frequently visited Stella and her companion, Rebecca, while Swift was in England. In a letter responding to Tisdall on the subject of a possible marriage between William and Stella, Swift admitted that if he had ever considered marriage, Stella would have been his first choice. "[I]f my fortunes and humour served me to think of that state [marriage], I should certainly, among all persons on earth, make your choice," Swift wrote Tisdall, "because I never saw that person whose conversation I entirely valued but her's." Swift did not openly discourage William and Stella from getting married, but he did not encourage them either. In the end, Tisdall married another woman.

Two months later, Swift was back in Ireland. He did not return to England for the next three and a half years. His cousin Thomas, writing to his father Deane Swift, wondered if Swift had a reason for staying so long in Ireland, asking mischievously "whether Jonathan be married? or whether he has been able to resist the charms of both those gentlewomen that marched quite from Moore-Park to Dublin (as they would have marched to the north or any where else) with full resolution to engage him?" To all appearances, though, Swift was uninterested in marriage. The relationship between Swift and Stella did not change.

Swift did have financial concerns. His income was barely enough to cover his personal expenses. He spent money on his parish as well, and he also helped support the ladies in Dublin. In a 1706 letter to John Temple, Sir William Temple's nephew, he identified his financial woes with those of Ireland, complaining, "If I love Ireland better than I did, it is because we are nearer related, for I am deeply allyed to it's Poverty. My little Revenue is sunk two Parts in three, and the third in Arrear."

Swift wrote very little during this time in Ireland. The poems and essays that he did produce showed his continuing interest in wordplay and puns. Although cut off from England's political scene, he maintained his interest in political issues, as he reflected on how English laws were hurting Ireland's economy. The Irish had been particularly devastated by laws preventing the export of any goods that competed with English manufacturing. Swift called attention to the issue in an essay called *The Story of the Injured Lady,* which was published in 1707. The story is an allegory in which an abusive man, symbolizing England, mistreats a woman, who represents Ireland.

That same year, Swift journeyed once more to England, but this time with the possibility of advancing both his political and religious careers. In Ireland, he had become good friends with Henry Herbert, the Earl of Pembroke. As lord lieutenant, Herbert served as the head of English administration of Ireland. In 1707, there was a major political controversy in England and Ireland over the question of a tax on Irish clerical incomes. The Anglican Church in Ireland was required to pay this tax, known as the First Fruits. However, since 1701 the clerical incomes for the Church of England had been exempt. Because the Church of Ireland was in extreme financial straits, the Irish clergy wanted Queen Anne to grant them the same exemption.

Swift was a clergyman with experience in English politics. He had also spent a good deal of time assuring Archbishop King that he was one of his strongest supporters. As a result, the archbishop decided Swift should represent the Church of Ireland in requesting the elimination of the First Fruits tax in Ireland. Along with the Earl of Pembroke, he sailed for England in November 1707.

While journeying to London, Swift stopped for a meal at an inn in the town of Dunstable. There, he encountered a family from Dublin, the Van Homrighs. Swift moved in the same social circles as the Van Homrighs, and he probably knew the family already. Among the four Van Homrigh children was a nineteen-year-old woman named Esther. Her father, who had died a few years earlier, had been a prominent figure in Dublin politics. While Swift dined with the family at the Dunstable inn, Esther spilled her coffee, which led to a conversation with Swift. In London, where Swift got to know the Van Homrighs better, he became closer to Esther and began to refer to her by the nickname Vanessa.

Esther Van Homrigh was of far superior birth to Stella. She also was intimately familiar with the politics of London and capable of conversing with Swift as an equal. Some scholars suggest that Swift's nickname for her, Vanessa, was derived from a shortening of her last name. (National Gallery of Ireland)

Swift's first priority in London, however, was the First Fruits mission. Despite his efforts, he soon found that no one else seemed to be interested. A lack of cooperation from the Church of Ireland also hindered him. He needed information from Ireland about the income of the Irish clergy, but these details were slow in coming. In February, Swift wrote impatiently to Archbishop King, "I have been above a Month expecting the Representation [of the Irish clergy's finances] your Grace was pleased to promise to send me, which makes me apprehend your Grace hath been hindered by . . . the Clergy's Backwardness in a Point so very necessary to their Service." Swift finally set a deadline, saying "If I have no Directions from your Grace by the End of this Month, I shall think of my Return to Ireland against the 25th of March, to endeavour to be chosen to the Living of St Nicholas, as I have been encouraged to hope."

The position in Ireland that Swift mentioned in this letter, however, was not forthcoming. Nor did Swift get very far with the First Fruits mission. Although he managed to speak with some influential Whig politicians, none of them gave him any significant help.

As he tried to further his cause, Swift heard a rumor that the Whigs would help support elimination of the First Fruits tax in Ireland if the Test Act was also abolished. Passed in 1673, the Test Act required anyone seeking a civil or military position to take a vow supporting the practices of the Anglican Church. The law essentially prevented Catholics and Nonconformists from holding political positions in England. Because of his strong belief in the

Anglican Church, Swift supported the Test Act. Writing to Dean Stearne, the head of St. Patrick's in Dublin, Swift made clear his opposition to repeal of the law:

> I beg you will endeavour among you, that the Church of Ireland gentlemen may send an address to set the Queen and Court right about the Test, which every one here is of opinion you should do; or else I have reason to fear it will be repealed here next session; which will be of terrible consequence, both as to the thing and the manner, by the parliament here interfering in things purely of Ireland, that have no relation to any interest of theirs.

This letter showed that, although Swift considered himself to be English in most ways, he was also very protective of Ireland, particularly its religious interests.

Although frustrated by the lack of progress with the First Fruits mission, Swift did not consider his time in London wasted. By 1708 he had become a well-known figure in the London literary scene. His popularity was due in part to friends such as the Van Homrighs who introduced him into society. But he also gained attention because of his fiery and witty style of writing.

While in London, Swift befriended the English writer Joseph Addison, a Whig who was chief secretary to the Earl of Wharton, the new lord lieutenant of Ireland. The Earl of Wharton had replaced Swift's friend, the Earl of Pembroke. Although the friendship between Addison and Swift would not last, at its outset Addison had great regard for his new

Joseph Addison, writer and politician, founded the Spectator *with his friend Richard Steele. The two shared a brief friendship with Swift that, like most of his relationships, was shortened by diverging political views.* (National Portrait Gallery)

friend. He gave Swift a copy of his book *Travels in Italy*, after inscribing a dedication in which he called Swift "the most Agreeable Companion, the Truest friend and the Greatest Genius of his Age."

Through Addison, Swift became friends with Richard Steele, another Dubliner by birth. Steele had gone to school with Addison and worked with him on at least one play. As editor of the *London Gazette*, Steele headed a major government newspaper. With some help from Swift, Steele also founded a weekly paper called the *Tatler*.

Although Swift played only a minor role in publishing the *Tatler*, the paper evolved from a series of satiric pamphlets Swift wrote called the *Bickerstaff Papers.* Writing under the false name Isaac Bickerstaff, Swift parodied the almanac of a popular astrologer named Partridge. Because Partridge's almanac often attacked the Anglican Church, Swift disliked it. Partridge's almanac also contained yearly predictions that he claimed were based on magic and the influence of the stars. In the *Bickerstaff Papers,* Swift published his own predictions.

In January 1708, the first set of *Bickerstaff Papers* was called *Predictions for the Year 1708.* One of the first predictions was "but a Trifle," the fictional Bickerstaff wrote. "It relates to Partridge the Almanack-Maker; I have consulted the Star of his Nativity by my own Rules; and find he will infallibly die upon the 29th of March next, about eleven at Night, of a raging Fever." Bickerstaff also predicted the deaths of others whom Swift considered to be enemies of the Anglican Church.

Partridge, unlike many readers, was not amused at the popular parody. He had no idea that Swift was the real author, and suspected another writer of the hoax. A few months later, Swift went on to write another Bickerstaff pamphlet in which he described the deathbed scene of the unfortunate astrologer. In a letter to a friend in Ireland, a furious Partridge denied the false report of his death:

> I dont doubt but you are Imposed on in Ireland also
> by a pack of Rogues about my being dead. . . . I thank

god I am very well in health, and at the time he had
doom'd me to death, I was not in the Least out of
order. . . . [Bickerstaff] knows nothing of Astrology,
but hath a good stock of Impudence and Lying.

The often cruel Bickerstaff pamphlets were typical of
Swift. He believed he was justified in his methods because
he was defending his principles and his church. Published
as an ongoing series, the *Bickerstaff Papers* became so
popular that soon the success of anything carrying the
Bickerstaff name was guaranteed. Steele and Addison also
wrote some Bickerstaff pamphlets for the *Tatler*. In one
issue of the paper, Steele thanked Swift, "whose pleasant
Writings, in the Name of Bickerstaff, created an Inclination
in the Town towards any Thing that could appear in the same
Disguise."

While works like the *Bickerstaff Papers* found an appre-
ciative audience with the Van Homrighs and others in their
social circle, Swift was also writing on other topics. In
Argument against Abolishing Christianity, published in
1708, he used masterful irony in inventing disputes with
writers who had attacked religion in the past, as he
argued for preservation of the Christian faith.

During the winter of 1708–1709, Swift's health wors-
ened. He struggled with symptoms of Menière's disease and
complained of "a cruel Distemper, a Giddiness in my Head,
that would not suffer me to write or think of any Thing."
At the time, no one knew how to treat the illness.

By March 1709, Swift saw that his First Fruits mission
was going nowhere. That month he wrote to Archbishop

King again about "the Proceedings in this unhappy Affair," and began considering a return to Ireland. Swift had other reasons for going back to Ireland. His friend Joseph Addison was leaving for Dublin with his employer, the Earl of Wharton. As chief secretary to the earl, Addison offered to help Swift find a good position there. Swift also recognized that his living expenses would be much less in Ireland than they were in England.

Swift said his goodbyes in London and left for Leicester, where he visited his mother. Whenever he had traveled to England in the past, he had stopped on his way to and from London to visit her. But now her health was very poor, and this meeting would be their last.

That June, Swift landed at Ringsend, Ireland, and immediately went home to Laracor. A few days later, he met up with Addison in Dublin. His friend had been eager to see him while in Ireland, writing "I think it is very hard I shou'd be in [th]e same Kingdome with Dr Swift and not have the Happinesse of his Company once in three days." During the time that Swift and Addison both spent in Ireland, Addison wrote to him more than once, asking for "the satisfaction and Honour of Dr. Swift's Conversation" in Dublin.

In the spring of 1710, while Swift was in Ireland, his mother died. Although they had never had a close relationship, he was deeply saddened by her death. He wrote, "I have now lost my barrier between me and death; God grant I may live to be as well prepared for it, as I confidently believe her to have been! If the way to Heaven be through piety, truth, justice, and charity, she is there."

Swift did not remain in Ireland for long. The Church of Ireland had not given up on the First Fruits mission, and that autumn Archbishop King gave Swift another opportunity to argue the case for the Irish clergy. Swift arrived in London at the beginning of September 1710, during a time of political upheaval. After many years in power,

Swift commissioned his friend Charles Jervas to paint a picture for Stella and her companion Rebecca Dingle. Jervas painted several pictures of Swift over the course of his career. This painting may have been presented to Stella or to another lady friend, Lady Betty Germaine. (Courtesy of the Granger Collection.)

the Whig-dominated government was falling. Within days of Swift's arrival, many leading Whigs lost their positions and Queen Anne replaced them with Tories.

Although some of these Whig officials were friends, Swift kept his distance from them, placing the interests of his career ahead of any personal preferences. In a letter to Stella he confided that they "would lay hold on me as a twig while they are drowning, and the great men making me their clumsy apologies." He added, "Every Whig in great office will, to a man, be infallibly put out; and we shall have such a winter as has not been seen in England."

Swift, who for so long would not side with one party or another, was now heading toward a firm alliance with the Tories, who were gaining political power under Queen Anne. Although some people criticized him for turning from the Whigs to the Tories, he had good reason to change his political allegiance. The Whigs had not helped him with the First Fruits issue or with the advancement of his career. Most important to Swift, the Whigs did not share his belief that the Anglican Church's authority should be supreme and unchallenged. He decided that the Tories better represented his interests in protecting the Anglican Church and improving the political systems that governed England and Ireland.

Swift now turned to Robert Harley, who was a moderate Tory and had just been appointed chancellor of the Exchequer, a position with responsibility for all financial matters of the government. Like Swift, Harley had once supported the Whigs, and the two men also shared a love of literature.

Robert Harley was a prominent patron of the arts. Swift and many others owed much of their success to his support. Swift repaid Harley's kindness by saving him from an assassination attempt in the form of a hat box rigged with loaded pistols. (National Portrait Gallery)

At one of their first meetings, Harley pleased Swift by quoting from one of his poems. Writing to Stella in Dublin, Swift optimistically reported, "I am already represented to Harley as a discontented person, that was used ill for not being Whig enough; and I hope for good usage from him."

With the help of Harley, Swift soon resolved the First Fruits issue. In his *Memoirs Relating to That Change which happened in the Queen's Ministry in the Year 1710,* he described the rapid course of events: "upon shewing my commission, [Harley] immediately undertook to perform it, which he accordingly did in less than three weeks, having settled it at five meetings with the Queen."

Grateful to Harley for his help, Swift was more than happy to accept a position offered by the new chancellor of the Exchequer. According to Swift's *Memoirs,* Harley told him "That the Queen was resolved to employ none but those who were friends to the constitution of church and state: That their great difficulty lay in the want of some good pen, to keep up the spirit raised in the people, to assert the principles, and justify the proceedings of the new ministers."

No writer was in a better position to provide "some good pen" for the new Tory administration than Swift. In October 1710, he became the editor of the *Examiner*, a weekly paper presenting the viewpoints of the Tories. As was his custom, he edited and wrote for the paper without using his own name, preferring to remain anonymous.

Although his friendship and interests were now with the Tories, Swift still viewed himself as a man of the Anglican Church, not one of any specific political party. He did not want anyone to think that the Tories had hired him. In his first article for the *Examiner*, in November 1710, he wrote, "It is a Practice I have generally followed, to converse in equal Freedom with the deserving Men of both Parties." He refused to be bought, as he saw it.

Swift liked and admired Robert Harley, but there were limits to friendship. Once, Harley sent fifty British pounds toward Swift's expenses and as payment for the work he was doing. It was meant as a kind and helpful gesture, but Swift was insulted and returned the money. Harley's unwelcome gift irritated him. "Mr Harley desired I would dine with him again today; but I refused him," he informed Stella, "for I fell out with him yesterday, and will not see him again till he makes me amends." The two men later resolved the quarrel.

Swift continued to write for the *Examiner* until mid-1711. He used his position at the paper to explain the changes in Queen Anne's government, to criticize Whig bishops in the Anglican Church, and to attack Whig politicians.

In addition to his work for the *Examiner,* Swift wrote other political pamphlets for Tory leaders Robert Harley and Henry St. John. One of the most influential was *The Conduct of the Allies and of the late ministry in beginning and carrying on the present war,* published in 1711. This pamphlet called for an end to the conflict known as the War of the Spanish Succession, which had begun in 1701. England had entered the war to limit French expansion, but Swift believed hostilities had been unnecessarily prolonged by the Whigs for political reasons. Swift's pamphlet proved to be very influential in Parliament. As the politicians debated how to bring about peace, they used the ideas and arguments set out in *The Conduct of the Allies.*

Another pamphlet by Swift, published in 1712, was entitled *A Proposal for Correcting, Improving, and Ascertaining the English Tongue.* In this work, the author suggested the establishment of an academy to institute a standard for the English language, which he believed was being degraded by the use of slang and bad grammar.

Between 1710 and 1713, Swift wrote detailed reports of his activities in England in his correspondence with Stella Johnson and Rebecca Dingley. These writings were later collected and published as *Journal to Stella*. In his letters, Swift described his political activities and worries, but he also wrote affectionately about the small details of his life, his dinners with friends and writers such as Joseph

One of Swift's many letters. This particular missive should have served as a warning to Vanessa of his vacillating affections and his embarrassment at having two lady admirers in the same country. (British Museum)

Aug. 12ª 1714   21.

I had yr Letter last Post, and before you can send me another, I shall set out for Ireld: I must go and take the Oaths, and the sooner the better. I think since I have known you I have drawn an old house upon my Head. You should not have come by Wantage for a thousand Pound. You used to brag you were very Discreet; where is it gone? It is probable I may not stey in Ireland long, but be back by the beginning of Winter. When I am there I will write to you as soon as I can conveniently, but it shall be always under a Cover; and if you write to me, let some other Direct it, and I beg you will write nothing that is particular, but what may be seen, for I apprehend Letters will be opened, and Inconveniences will happen. If you are in Ireld while I am there I shall see you very seldom. It is not a Place for any Freedom, but where every thing is known in a Week, and magnified a hundred Degrees. These are rigorous Laws that must be passed through: but it is probable we me meet in London in Winter, or if not, leave all to Fate, that seldom cares to humor our Inclinations.. I say all this out the perfect Esteem and Friendship I have for you. These Publick Misfortunes have altered all my Measures, and broke my Spirits. God Almighty bless you; I shall, I hope be on horseback in a day after

Addison and William Congreve, and his longing to see his friends in Ireland again.

In the correspondence between Swift and Stella, he refers to her as "MD," or "my dear," and uses other pet names. His letters often ran long, and to reduce the amount of paper needed to write them, Swift wrote in very small script. In one letter, he affectionately teased about the effect his tiny writing could have on its reader. "And can Stella read this writing without hurting her dear eyes? O, faith, I'm afraid not," he warned. "Have a care of those eyes, pray, pray, pretty Stella."

Swift was very open in his letters to Stella, and he often made merciless comments about people who annoyed or angered him. In one letter he regretfully informed Stella that Addison's allegiance to the Whigs had changed the relationship between the two friends. "I called at the coffeehouse, where I had not been in a week, and talked coldly a while with Mr Addison," he wrote. "[A]ll our friendship and dearness are off: we are civil acquaintance, talk words of course, of when we shall meet, and that's all."

Swift's correspondence also reflected his sense of humor, as he complained to Stella how hard it was to find transportation in the city whenever it rained. "I am here in a pretty pickle: it rains hard; and the cunning natives of Chelsea have outwitted me, and taken up all the three stagecoaches," he told her. In his letters, he requested news on his home in Ireland. "Have I any apples at Laracor?" he once asked, and then commented, "It is strange every year should blast them, when I took so much care for shelter."

Through Swift's letters, Stella comes across as his most treasured correspondent.

During this stay in London, Swift renewed his efforts to obtain an important clerical position in England. Once again his ambitions were dashed. Although Swift now had powerful friends in London, Queen Anne was not among them. She knew Swift had authored *A Tale of a Tub,* and had found the pamphlet offensive. The Queen did not want to reward Swift by giving him a position within the Church of England. However, she was willing to give him an opportunity in Ireland, as dean of St. Patrick's Cathedral in Dublin.

When first offered the position as dean of St. Patrick's, Swift was disappointed. He wrote to Stella, "[The] Lord-Treasurer . . . told me the Queen was at last resolved, that Dr Sterne should be Bishop of Dromore, and I Dean of St Patrick's . . . I do not know whether it will yet be done; some unlucky accident may yet come. Neither can I feel joy at passing my days in Ireland."

But no accident came to prevent the appointment, and Swift went back to Dublin in June 1713 to take up the position of dean. *Journal to Stella* ends there, with one last letter to the ladies sent from Chester, a stop on the journey to Holyhead, the port town in Wales where Swift boarded the ship that took him to Ireland. "[P]erhaps I may be with you in a week." he wrote Stella. "I will be three days going to Holyhead; I cannot ride faster. . . . I am upon Stay-behind's mare."

Despite being granted the prestigious position, Swift

did not want to live in Ireland. Even before going back to the land of his birth, he wrote glumly to a friend: "I am condemned to live again in Ireland, and all that the Court or Ministry did for me, was to let me chuse my Station in the Country where I am banished." Soon after his return to Dublin, his discontented feelings with the country of his birth also returned. After the ceremony installing him as dean of St. Patrick's, he returned to Laracor, ill with vertigo.

In July, he wrote to Vanessa that his health had improved, most likely because he was in Laracor rather than Dublin. "I am riding here for life, and think I am something better," he stated. "[I] hate the Thoughts of Dublin, and prefer a field-bed and an Earthen floor before the great House there."

Vanessa wrote to Swift often while he was in Laracor, urging him to return to England. He was reluctant to answer her letters, wondering if their close friendship had led her to expect more from their relationship than he was willing to give. When he finally did write back to her, he made it clear that he might not come back to England. "[N]either will I leave the Kingdom [of Ireland] till I am sent for, and if they have no further service for me, I will never see England again," he declared.

Within a short time, however, Swift changed his mind. That September he returned to London. Not wanting anyone to think he was too happy anywhere, Swift quickly wrote to a friend. "I protest I am less fond of Engl^d than ever," he insisted. This visit would be his last long stay in England.

CHAPTER FIVE

Literary London, Dirty Dublin

Upon his return to London in the fall of 1713, Jonathan Swift plunged back into the intellectual and political life of the city. Soon he was writing his friend Archdeacon Thomas Walls that he was growing "heartily weary of Courts, and Ministries, and politicks." English politics wore him down; he was torn between the interests of those he considered his friends, and the best interests of the Church.

Swift grew concerned about a major division that had developed within the Tory government. The rift involved two important Tory leaders—Swift's old friend Robert Harley, who was now the Earl of Oxford, and Henry St. John, also known as Viscount Bolingbroke. The two men disagreed over many aspects of government policy. Harley was more willing to compromise with the Whigs and their moderate religious views, while St. John was a hard-line

Tory, determined to preserve the purity of the Church.

Swift sympathized with Harley but preferred St. John's politics. To show his support for Harley as a friend, Swift wrote at least two poems praising him and his family around this time. But he disagreed with his old friend's political approach. "For in your publick Capacity you have often angred me to the Heart," he wrote to Harley, "but as a private man never once."

Both Harley and St. John were in contact with Queen Anne's half-brother, James Francis Edward Stuart, a son of the deposed king James II. Sometimes referred to as the Old Pretender, or even James III, he had gone into exile in France in 1688, where he plotted a return to England to seize the crown. Dealings with him were considered to be treasonable offenses against Queen Anne's government.

Swift did not know anything about Harley and St. John's discussions with Stuart. He tried to mend the relations between the two men, but the Tory government had already become unstable. Queen Anne was in poor health, and the likelihood of her death made the political future of the Tory party uncertain.

Swift found some compensation for the frustrations of English politics, though. In early 1714, he formed a literary club with John Arbuthnot, the Queen's doctor. Arbuthnot also enjoyed writing satire. When Swift wrote his political pamphlet *The Conduct of the Allies*, Arbuthnot wrote a similarly successful satire on the same subject entitled *The History of John Bull*. Other members of the new club

St. James's Palace, meeting place of the Scriblerus Club, as it looked during the reign of Queen Anne. (Courtesy of the Granger Collection.)

included the writers Alexander Pope and John Gay, as well as Thomas Parnell, an Irish poet who lived in London. The members met in coffeehouses or at St. James's Palace, the official residence of the queen and the government administrative center, where Arbuthnot lived. The meetings at St. James's Palace also allowed Robert Harley to join them occasionally, but he was not at club meetings as often as the members would have liked. Swift once wrote a poem to Harley that included a request that he join the group more often:

> The Doctor and Dean, Pope, Parnell and Gay
> In manner submissive most humbly do pray,

That your Lordship would once let your cares all alone
And climb the dark stairs to your friends who have none.

The writers called their new group the Scriblerus Club. Among their goals was to write a biography of Martin Scriblerus, a fictional character who dabbled in every field, but succeeded in none of them. Years later Alexander Pope explained the purpose of writing a biography on a nonexistent person. "The design of the Memoirs of Scriblerus," he wrote, "was to have ridiculed all the false tastes in learning, under the character of a man of capacity enough,

Coffeehouses often functioned as meeting places for intellectuals. Like the members of the Scriblerus Club, they came together to debate and encourage one another in literary and artistic pursuits. (Courtesy of Art Resource.)

that had dipped into every art and science, but injudiciously in each." Although the writing of the Scriblerus biography did not go very far, the members of his club enjoyed themselves by staying up late, eating and drinking, and writing silly poems.

On the more serious side, Swift continued writing about political issues. Political differences with his friend Joseph Addison, an avid Whig, had destroyed the relationship between the two men. Swift's friendship with Richard Steele, also a strong Whig supporter, also ended bitterly and in a more public forum. Before Swift left for Ireland in the summer of 1713, Steele had started a new publication, called the *Guardian*. Although the *Guardian* was supposed to be a neutral paper, offering the viewpoints of both political parties, Steele began using it to attack the *Examiner*. Because Swift was the chief writer and editor for the *Examiner*, he took Steele's attacks personally and wrote some angry letters to his former friend.

Upon Swift's return to London in September 1713, Steele started up yet another paper, which he called the *Englishman*. Unlike the *Guardian*, this paper did not try to be neutral. It openly supported the Whigs. Along with some other Whigs, Steele also produced a pamphlet called *The Crisis*, which appeared in January 1714. This pamphlet discussed English history at length and argued that the descendants of the Catholic James II presented a threat to Protestant succession to the throne of England. Steele dedicated the pamphlet to the English clergy, but he also went further. He suggested that clergy members read the pamphlet in church and modify their preaching to match its views.

Swift disagreed with the Whig opinions that Steele expressed in *The Crisis*. He had a response ready for publication only one month after the appearance of *The Crisis*. Published anonymously, the document was entitled *The Public Spirit of the Whigs: Set Forth in their Generous Encouragement of the Author of The Crisis: With Some Observations on the Seasonableness, Candor, Erudition, and Style of that Treatise.*

Richard Steele was suspended from parliament for his pamphlet's outspoken support of George of Hanover for succession to the British throne instead of any of the Catholic descendants of the currently ruling Stuart family. He and other Whigs thought it better to have a German king than a Catholic one. (Courtesy of the Granger Collection.)

Swift began *The Public Spirit* with a dig at Steele's writing style, using heavy sarcasm to express his bitter disapproval of the Whig while pretending to praise him. For example, he stated that Steele has "Qualities enough to denominate him a Writer of a superior Class . . . provided he would a little regard the Propriety and Disposition of his Words, consult the Grammatical Part, and get some Information in the Subject he intends to handle." Later, in referring to *The Crisis*, Swift asked, "What shall I say to a Pamphlet, where the Malice and Falshood of every Line would require an Answer, and where the Dulness and Absurdities will not deserve one?"

Scholars today consider *The Public Spirit of the Whigs* one of Swift's greatest political pamphlets. In it, Swift precisely identifies the many contradictions and inconsistencies in his former friend's arguments. The pamphlet even questions Steele's loyalty to England. "The Author of the *Crisis* may be fairly proved from his own Citations to be guilty of HIGH TREASON," Swift's political pamphlet declares. It also accuses Steele of undermining the confidence of the English people in their Queen. Swift concludes his political pamphlet by stating, "Whoever writes at this Rate of his Sovereign, to whom he owes so many personal Obligations, I should never enquire whether he be a GENTLEMAN BORN, but whether he be a HUMAN CREATURE."

Although *The Public Spirit of the Whigs* effectively demolished Steele's arguments, the pamphlet caused trouble for Swift as well. It had a strong anti-Scottish tone and suggested Scots should not be represented in Parliament. (This was controversial because the 1707 Act of Union had officially united the nations of Scotland and England and established a single governmental body, the parliament of Great Britain.) When Swift's pamphlet became public, Scottish members of parliament called for its author and the publishers to be taken to court. Swift had a new edition published with the paragraph about the Scots taken out, but the damage had already been done.

Because the inflammatory pamphlet was published anonymously, authorities could arrest only its printer and publisher. The Queen agreed to offer a reward of three hundred British pounds to anyone who could discover the author's identity. Harley, the earl of Oxford, worried about his friend's safety. He sent Swift some money to bail out the publisher and printer, along with a note in disguised handwriting. "I have heard that some honest men who are very innocent are under troble touching a Printed pamphlet," Harley cautiously wrote. He explains, without naming names, that "a friend of mine, an obscure person, but charitable, puts the enclosed Bill in y^r hands to answer such exigencys as their case may immediatly require."

The fuss died down after a while, but Swift found himself tiring of the never-ending political crises in England. In a letter to his friend the Earl of Peterborough, he wrote, "I assure you, my Lord, for the concern I have for the common cause, with relation to affairs both at home and abroad, and from the personal love I bear to our friends in power, I never led a life so thoroughly uneasy as I do at present."

Aware that the Tory government would fall after the death of Queen Anne, who by now was quite ill, Swift decided to leave London. However, he was not quite ready to return to Ireland. In June 1714, he went to visit his friend the Reverend John Geree, who lived in the Berkshire countryside. In a letter to Vanessa, written only a week after he arrived in Berkshire, Swift wrote affectionately of Geree: "I am at a Clergyman's house, an old Friend and Acquaintance, whom I love very well, but he is such a melancholy thoughtfull man, partly from Nature, and partly by a solitary Life, that I shall soon catch the Spleen from Him."

But there was no doubt that Swift preferred to be away from London. Archdeacon Walls, in Dublin, received a letter around the same time in which Swift described how tired he felt. "I am now retired into the Country weary to death of Courts and Ministers, and Business and Politicks," Swift wrote. "I care not to live in Storms, when I can no longer do Service in the ship, and am able to get out of it." For Swift, the death of the queen would signal the end of all that he had worked for in England. The dominance of the Tories would cease, along with the advantages of the Tory government for the Anglican Church.

On August 1, 1714, Queen Anne died. She was succeeded by George I, a descendent of James I from the German house of Hanover. Erasmus Lewis, an important Tory politician who had been the under-secretary of state, wrote to Swift on August 3: "I . . . think you sh'd come to town to see how the world goes. for all old schemes designs projects journey's, &c: are broke by the great event." Henry St. John also urged Swift not to leave England. "Pray don't go," he pleaded. "I am against it, but that is nothing. . . . Ireland will be the scene of some disorder. . . . here every thing is quiet & will continue so. besides which as prosperity divided, misfortunes may perhaps to some degree unite us."

Swift knew that with the death of Queen Anne, St. John's political power would soon diminish, as would that of the other major Tory politicians. In his reply to St. John, Swift tried to stay positive, but he admitted, "We have certainly more heads and hands than our adversaries; but, it must be confessed, they have stronger shoulders and better hearts."

A few days later, St. John wrote again. "Go into Ireland, since it must be so," he said, "& come back into Brittain to bless. To bless me and those few friends who will enjoy you." In fact, Swift had no choice about going back to Ireland, at least for a while. As the dean of St. Patrick's, he had to be in Dublin to take formal oaths of allegiance to the new king.

However, one last drama remained in store for Swift before he left for Ireland. In the first week after Queen Anne's death, Vanessa arrived unexpectedly at Wantage, a village near where Swift was staying. No one knows exactly what she said to Swift, but judging from the tone of the letter that he wrote to her a few days later, he felt threatened by her sudden arrival. "You should not have come by Wantage for a thousand Pound," he rebuked her. "You used to brag you were very discreet; where is it gon[e]?"

Swift continued his letter by informing Vanessa that he would soon leave for Ireland, and that if she planned to write to him there, she had to be careful about what her letters said. "It is not a Place for any Freedom, but where ever[y] thing is known in a Week, and magnifyed a hundred Degrees," he warned. "I say all this out [of] the perfect Esteem and Friendship I have for You." But then Swift ended his letter abruptly, refusing to address all the points in her previous letter to him. "I would not answer your Questions for a Million," he said. "[N]or can I think of them with any Ease of Mind. adieu."

Since Vanessa and Swift had grown close over the past several years, the questions almost certainly had to do with the nature of their relationship, and what she could expect from him in the future. Swift either did not fully understand the effect that he had on the young women in his life, or he did not really care about the impressions that his words and actions left. He would not answer Vanessa's questions. As far as he was concerned, her expectations were neither his fault nor his problem.

In a poem written for Vanessa around 1713, called "Cadenus and Vanessa," Swift tells the story of a highly intelligent man who is loved by a beautiful and talented woman. However, because the man cannot understand love, he cannot return it: "He now could praise, esteem, approve, / But understood not what was love." The story is loosely based on Greek mythology, but the identies of the characters Swift is writing about are obvious. Vanessa even called Swift by the name Cadenus, or Cad, in some of the letters that they exchanged. In the poem, Swift wants Vanessa to realize that he admires her, but that he cannot commit to her.

By August 24, Swift was back in Dublin. Depressed by once again having to take up life in Ireland, he wrote to his friend Charles Ford, "I know not what to say to You. I cannot think or write in this Country. . . . I hope I shall keep my Resolution of never medling with Irish Politicks. . . . Being in Eng^d onely renders this Place more hatefull to me, which Habitude would make tolerable." A letter to Matthew Prior, one of his Tory friends, in March 1715 contained the bleak request: "Will you tell our Friends that I am just alive, and that is all."

Swift set about arranging his official residence in Dublin, the Deanery, to his satisfaction. That included, as he wrote humorously to his friend Knightley Chetwode, removing the former dean's household pet. "One occasion I have to triumph," Swift reported, "that in six weeks time I have been able to get rid of a great Cat, that belonged to the late Dean, and almost poisoned the house." In another letter written two weeks later, he could not resist adding that the cat "by her perpetual noise and stink must be certainly a Whig."

Life as dean of St. Patrick's Cathedral in Dublin, Ireland, paled in comparison to the hectic literary and political life Swift had experienced in London. He explained to his friend Alexander Pope, "You are to understand that I live in the corner of a vast unfurnished house, . . . and when I

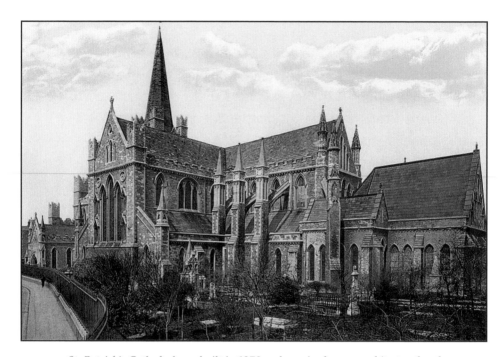

St. Patrick's Cathedral was built in 1270 and survived many architectural and religious revisions. Swift served as dean of the cathedral between 1713 and 1745. Handel's Messiah *was first performed at the cathedral in 1742.* (Library of Congress)

do not dine abroad, or make an entertainment, (which last is very rare) I eat a mutton-pye, and drink half a pint of wine." His challenges, Swift continued, consisted of "defending my small dominions against the Arch-Bishop, and endeavouring to reduce my rebellious Choir."

As the dean of one of Ireland's most important and powerful cathedrals, Swift was determined to assert his authority and to make sure that Archbishop King did not take control of areas that Swift considered his rightful territory. In addition to getting caught up in the semipolitical struggles within his cathedral and the Church of Ireland, Swift also had to do some preaching. Although he was a clergyman, Swift spent more time writing on politics and literature than theology. Even his most passionate sermons usually had a political dimension.

Swift delivered one of his most famous sermons, "On Brotherly Love," in December 1717 from the pulpit of St. Patrick's. After insisting that "there is no Duty more incumbent upon those who profess the Gospel, than that of Brotherly Love," he thundered against "the Papists and Fanaticks, who each, in their Turns, filled [Ireland] with Blood and Slaughter, and for a Time destroyed both the Church and the Government." He also bemoaned the forces that divided men, including political disagreements and the desire for power. His sermons spoke of the conflicts in his own life, including the struggles for power within his cathedral of St. Patrick's.

Swift was also struggling with decisions in his personal life. Vanessa Van Homrigh was not content to stay in England and exchange the occasional "discreet" letter with Swift. Less than two months after his departure from England, the impetuous young woman left for Ireland. She settled in Celbridge, near Dublin, where her father had left her a large estate. Because Stella was also in Ireland, Vanessa's presence placed Swift in an awkward position.

In his first letter to Vanessa after her arrival, Swift did not tell her that she should not have come, but her actions clearly aggravated him. "I would not have gone to Kildrohod [Celbridge] to see you for all the World," he stated. "I ever told you, you wanted [lacked] Discretion." Swift also discouraged Vanessa from finding much to like about

Ireland. "Pray take Care of your health in this Irish air to which You are a Stranger," he warned. "Does not Dublin look very dirty to You, and the Country very miserable." However, he agreed to visit her regularly—though as secretly as possible—at her town lodgings in Dublin.

Not surprisingly, Vanessa was confused by Jonathan's vacillating behavior. Sometimes Swift talked like a man in love. Once, he wrote a letter to Vanessa in shaky French, telling her that she possessed every virtue, and that he placed her above every other woman in the human race. At other times, he pushed Vanessa away.

Swift was afraid of the impression that the parishioners of St. Patrick's might get if they learned of his relationship with Vanessa. On one occasion at least, he was alarmed by the gossip that was going around. "This morning a Woman who does Business for me, told me she heard I was in—with one—naming you," he wrote Vanessa. "I ever feared the Tattle of this nasty Town; and I told you so; and that was the Reason why I said to you long ago that I would see you seldom when you were in [Ireland]. and I must beg you to be easy if for some time I visit you seldomer."

But Vanessa, in turn, felt very insecure in Ireland. She begged Swift to visit her more often, to come see her in Celbridge, and to stop tormenting her. "[T]is impossible to discribe what I have suffer'd since I saw you last," Vanessa wrote to Swift. "I am sure I could have bore the Rack, much better than those killing, killing, words of yours. some times I have resolved to die without seeing you more. . . . oh that you may but have so much regard for me left that this complaint may touch your soul with pitty."

Vanessa was not the only woman in Swift's life. He continued to maintain his friendship with Stella. Both women were often in Dublin at the same time, but Swift kept

Stella, as she looked in Dublin. Stella benefited from Vanessa's proximity. The contrast between Vanessa's disposition, which became more violently passionate as Swift's indecision wore on, and her own sweetly compliant nature won Swift's undying affection. (National Gallery of Ireland)

his relationship with each separate. Still, they certainly knew of each other's existence. Several Swift biographers believe that Swift actually married Stella, in 1716, but no solid proof exists. Nor is there any evidence that she pressured Swift about the nature of their relationship. Like Vanessa, though, Stella received some poems dedicated to her. For her thirty-eighth birthday, Swift coyly disregarded her real age and wrote:

> Stella this day is thirty-four,
> (We shan't dispute a year or more:)
> However Stella, be not troubled,
> Although thy size and years are doubled,
> Since first I saw thee at sixteen,
> The brightest virgin on the green.
> So little is thy form declined;
> Made up so largely in thy mind.

In addition to his women friends, Swift developed other friendships in Ireland. In 1718, he became good friends with Thomas Sheridan. Much younger than Swift, Sheridan was a schoolmaster who had also qualified to enter the Church as a clergyman. Like Swift, he loved to play with words and in 1719 published a book called *Art of Punning*. Many years later, after Sheridan's death, Swift wrote warmly about his friend's talents, describing him as "doubtless the best instructor of youth in these kingdoms, or perhaps in Europe." Swift was not as complimentary in describing Sheridan's ability as a writer: "His English verses were full of wit and humour, but neither his prose nor verse sufficiently correct: However, he would readily submit to any friend who had a true taste in prose or verse."

Although Swift enjoyed spending time with Sheridan, neither he nor Stella Johnson liked Sheridan's wife. In a letter to Sheridan signed by both Swift and Stella, they rejected an invitation to go to Sheridan's house. "Mrs. Dingley and Mrs. Johnson say, truly they don't care for your Wife's Company," the letter read, "tho' they like your Wine; but they had rather have it at their own House to drink in quiet." In Swift's essay *The History of the Second Solomon*, he writes about Sheridan (referred to by the nickname Solomon), and criticizes his friend because "he lets his wife (whom he pretends to hate as she deserves) govern, insult, and ruin him, as she pleases."

Another Irishman who befriended Swift around this time was Patrick Delany, whom Swift probably met through Thomas Sheridan. Like Sheridan, Delany was much younger than Swift, but age differences mattered little when Swift enjoyed someone for their intelligence and wit.

On one occasion, Delany helped to mend a rift between Swift and Sheridan when the latter overstepped the line in a playful exchange of comic poetry. Sheridan had written some verses describing Swift's funeral as being attended by owls and donkeys. Swift did not find Sheridan's joke funny and subsequently criticized the young writer's other work. "I have long thought severall of his Papers, and particularly that of the Funerall, to be out of all of the Rules of Raillery," Swift wrote about Sheridan to Delany. "And if you think the same you ought to tell him so in the manner you like best, without bringing me into the Question, else I may be thought a Man who will not take a Jest." Delany helped to resolve the matter, and all was well between the friends again.

In Dublin, Swift had soon gathered around him a group of young men who were aspiring writers and who enjoyed his sharp sense of humor. The group wrote mocking verses about their friends, discussed literature, and listened in fascination to Swift's stories. Swift enjoyed being the head of an admiring group but complained that by living in Ireland, he had lost his ability to write, as well as his fame. In 1719, he wrote to his friend St. John in England:

> If you will recollect that I am towards six years older than when I saw you last, and twenty years duller, you will not wonder to find me abound in empty speculations: I can now express in a hundred words what would formerly have cost me ten. . . . I have gone the round of all my stories three or four times with the younger people, and begin them again. I give hints how significant a person I have been, and no body believes me; I pretend to pity them, but am inwardly angry.

Many years later, Delany wrote a short biography of Swift that contained insights into his character, his relationships with others, and his feelings about Ireland. "The truth is," Delany said of Swift, "he considered Ireland as a scene too little for his genius." In fact, Swift was quite wrong to think that his life in Ireland would hinder his genius, or that he could not find the same savage inspiration there that had brought him fame in England. During the 1720s, while Swift considered himself to be "in exile" in Ireland, he would produce some of his greatest works. Many of them would be written on behalf of Ireland and the Irish, about whom he had such mixed feelings.

CHAPTER SIX

Irish Hero

Upon his arrival in Ireland in 1714, Swift could not have known that twelve years would pass before he saw England again. For the first several years of his residence in Dublin, he wrote very little, blaming his lack of inspiration on Ireland. In 1719, in a letter to his close friend Charles Ford, who was living in London, Swift apologized for his long literary silence. "It is really a difficult matter to be a good Correspondent from hence, where [there] is nothing materiall to say, where you know very few, and care for nothing that can pass in such a Scene as this, nor I neither if I could help it. . . . I do every thing to make me forget my self and the World as much as I can."

But Swift's fascination with his fellow human beings and with the political scene could not stay dormant forever. At the end of the same year, he wrote again to Ford and admitted a growing interest in Irish events. "[A]s the World is now turned," he said, "no Cloyster is retired enough to keep Politicks out, and I will own they raise my Passions whenever they come in my way, perhaps more than yours who live amongst them, as a great Noise is likelyer to disturb a Hermit than a Citizen." Swift began to realize that great changes in the political and social scenes could take place not only in England but also in Ireland.

For most of his life, Swift had felt much more at home in England than in Ireland. However, as the years passed, he slowly began to identify with the land where he had been born and raised. Increasingly disturbed by the extreme poverty and oppression that he saw all around him, Swift reached the point where he could no longer ignore the misery of the Irish people. He believed that the responsibility for much of their suffering could be laid at the door of the British government.

The leaders of Great Britain had determined that their needs would be served best if Ireland was governed as a colony. If Ireland became more prosperous than England and economically self-reliant, they reasoned, the English would lose their claim to Ireland's many resources. As a result, in 1720, the British parliament asserted England's domination by passing the Declaratory Act, also known as the "Sixth of George I," which declared that England had the right to pass laws that affected Ireland.

The British government decided to invest very little money in its "colony," to keep the Irish dependent on England, and to exploit Ireland in any way possible. One

Jonathan Swift, as the dean of St. Patrick's Cathedral, painted around 1718 by his friend, Charles Jervas. The pen and paper seem particularly appropriate to the man remembered more as a satirist than as a clergyman. (Courtesy of the Granger Collection.)

reason for this was that at the time, Great Britain was experiencing serious financial difficulties. Most of

England's economic troubles came about because of problems caused by the South Sea Company, which had been founded in 1711 by Swift's friend Robert Harley. In return for financial assistance and investment from the British government, the South Sea Company was given all trading rights with the Spanish colonies in South America, as well as other trading rights with Spain. The South Sea Company agreed to finance the British national debt and to pay the British government £7 million. The company could then invest the value of the debt in its overseas trading activities. Soon, investors were spending millions of pounds to buy South Sea Company stock, and the value of shares in the company rose enormously.

By 1720, South Sea Company stock shares had become tremendously overvalued. When investors learned about the shaky status of the company, panic selling caused the stock market to crash. This financial catastrophe, referred to as the South Sea Bubble, ruined many investors, who lost vast fortunes overnight. People were furious with the company and with the British government. Ireland also suffered, as some Irish investors experienced huge financial losses.

The South Sea Bubble aggravated the struggling economy in Ireland, which had been weakened by previous English laws. For example, a 1699 British law known as the Wool Act prevented the export of any woolen goods from Ireland to other countries except England. The Irish textile industry was also suffering because the wealthy Irish were purchasing English clothing and textiles, rather than

Edward Matthew Ward's rendering of the South Sea Bubble fiasco shows the naive consternation of the populace. (Courtesy of Art Resource.)

Irish manufactured goods. A sharp increase in poverty meant many poor Irish were living on the edge of starvation.

English landlords, or wealthy property owners who rented land to Irish farmers, caused an additional drain on the Irish economy. Most of them did not live in Ireland, and Swift once estimated that absentee landlords spent at least a third of the money received from Irish tenants in England. Many people believed that the English were using up Ireland's resources, taking away the small amount of money that Ireland had, and giving nothing back.

In May 1720, Swift believed it was time to comment on the deplorable state of the nation. With his political pamphlet *A Proposal for the Universal Use of Irish*

Manufacture, he broke his years of literary silence with a major statement on behalf of the Irish people. The short pamphlet was the first political work that he had published since 1714. In the document, Swift uses irony to criticize the English for oppressing the Irish, and the Irish for allowing the English to oppress them. "How grievously POOR ENGLAND suffers by Impositions from Ireland," he states with heavy sarcasm, ". . . That the Governing of this Kingdom costs the Lord Lieutenant three Thousand six Hundred Pounds a Year, so much net Loss to POOR ENGLAND. That the People of Ireland presume to dig for Coals in their own Grounds; and the Farmers in the County of Wicklow send their Turf to the very Market of Dublin, to the great Discouragement of the Coal Trade at Mostyn and White-haven."

At the same time, Swift also wondered why the Irish parliament continued to waste its time with irrelevant questions, instead of helping its people. "I SHOULD wish the parliament . . . , instead of those great Refinements in Politicks and Divinity, had amused Themselves and their Committees, a little, with the State of the Nation," he wrote.

Swift believed that the lot of the Irish people would improve a great deal if they increased their economic self-sufficiency by purchasing goods manufactured in Ireland, instead of England. Although he sided with the Irish against the English, he did not see the Irish simply as innocent victims. Rather, he was angry about their acceptance of oppression, and he urged the Irish to take action by not buying English goods.

Whether or not Swift's ideas actually offered a realistic solution to Ireland's desperate problems, the pamphlet caused quite a stir. Like most of his work, it was published anonymously. However, Swift's forceful and humorous style was too distinctive by now for him not to be suspected as the author. Only one month after the pamphlet's publication, a bishop in northern Ireland suggested its source in a letter written to a colleague: "There is so much of the Dean of St. Patrick's witty and bantering Strain in this Piece that the greatest part of its Readers (at the first Blush) give him the Honour of being its Author."

The pamphlet's printer, a Dubliner named Edward Waters, got into more trouble than its author, as was often the case when Swift published an inflammatory work. In an effort to help the printer, while not admitting openly that he was the author, Swift wrote to one of his influential friends, asking him to help Waters. "Now if the Chief Justice continues his Keenness," Swift worried, "the Man may be severely punished; but the Business may be inconvenient, because I am looked on as the Author." With the help of his powerful friends, Swift eventually managed to save the printer from imprisonment and ruin.

Judging from the outraged reaction that the pamphlet drew from many politicians, judges, and bishops in both England and Ireland, *A Proposal for the Universal Use of Irish Manufacture* was a strong piece of work. Swift was back with a vengeance.

Now in his fifties, Swift was not in the best health. Worried about the effects that his aging was having on his

Alexander Pope, member of the Scriblerus Club, suffered from Pott's disease, which never allowed him to grow over five feet. His best-known work, The Rape of the Lock, *is a witty satire in verse.* (Courtesy of the Granger Collection.)

writing abilities, he expressed his concerns in *A Letter from Dr. Swift to Mr. Pope*, published in 1721. The letter was never actually sent to Alexander Pope, since it was intended as a statement about Swift's ideas and his situation, rather than as a private letter. Swift wrote, "If my genius and spirit be sunk by encreasing years, I have at least enough discretion left, not to mistake the measure of my own abilities, by attempting subjects where those talents are necessary, which perhaps I may have lost with my youth." But it was obvious from the quality and content of his writing that his passion for justice and for the advancement of humanity was as strong as ever.

Unfortunately, Swift had a more difficult time understanding the passions in his personal life. Vanessa, who now lived mainly at Celbridge, continued to visit Dublin. She desperately begged Swift to visit her more often and to pay more attention to her. The young woman was lonely, especially after the death of her sister Mary from tuberculosis in 1721.

Swift had never answered Vanessa's questions about the nature of their relationship. In his letters, he put her off by joking about issues that were extremely serious to her. "You do not find I answer your Questions to your Satisfaction," he noted. "Prove to me first that it was ever possible to answer any thing to your satisfaction so as that you would not grumble in half an hour." At other times, he reminisced about the twelve years of their relationship, fondly remembering the incident that initiated their friendship "from the Time of spilling the Coffee to drinking of Coffee, from Dunstable to Dublin with every single passage since."

In July 1721, Swift finally suggested that Vanessa would be happier if she moved away from Ireland. "Shall you who have so much Honor and good Sense act otherwise to make Cad and your self miserable.— Settle your Affairs, and quit this scoundrel Island," he recommended, "and things will be as you desire." But Swift made no suggestion that he would follow if she left Ireland, which was what she wanted.

The last existing letters between Swift and Vanessa were written in 1722, while Swift was traveling by horseback on a vacation in northern Ireland. When Vanessa died a year later of tuberculosis—the same disease that had taken her sister's life—their long friendship had ended bitterly, and she left him nothing in her will.

Swift said nothing about Vanessa in letters written to friends after she died. However, in a letter to Knightley Chetwode written just a few hours after Vanessa's death, he said vaguely, "I am forced to leave the Town sooner than I expected." He then left Dublin to travel in the south of Ireland for a few months, apparently needing to get away for some time.

In the early 1720s, a new political and economic controversy was brewing in Ireland, which was enough to take Swift's mind off any personal problems and sadness that he was experiencing. In 1722, an Englishman named William Wood was granted a patent from the British government for the right to manufacture a new coin in Ireland that was made of an inexpensive metal—copper. Wood stood to make a huge profit from the new coins, which were referred to as Wood's Halfpence. However, the Irish government and people believed that the introduction of this cheap form of currency, which the British government was imposing on Ireland, could harm the nation's weak economy.

The new coins would also be useless outside of Ireland. By 1724, although the Irish parliament opposed the new currency, its introduction seemed almost certain.

Dismayed by this prospect, Swift decided that he had to speak for the people who would lose the most if the new currency was approved: the Irish lower classes. The first of his new series of political pamphlets, *The Drapier's Letters*, appeared in February 1724. Addressed "to the Tradesmen, Shop-Keepers, Farmers, and Country-People in General, of the Kingdom of IRELAND," Swift's letter claimed to be written by someone on the same social level as its intended audience: a man named M. B. Drapier. (A drapier, or draper, was a person who sold cloth.)

The actual worth of the metal in the new coin was far less than a halfpenny. Swift perceived that this discrepancy would destroy Ireland's feeble economy. His Drapier's Letters *and the people's discovery that William Wood only got the job by bribing the king's mistress spelled the end of Wood's Halfpence.* (British Museum)

Swift admitted to colleagues that he was the author of *The Drapier's Letters*. In April he wrote to Charles Ford, "I do not know wheth' I told you that I sent out a small Pamphlet under the Name of a Draper, laying the whole Vilany open, and advising People what to do." Still, the author remained pessimistic about how much good the pamphlets would accomplish in Ireland. "About 2000 of them have been dispersd by Gentlemen in severall Parts of the Country," Swift explained, "but one can promise nothing from such Wretches as the Irish People."

Even though he wrote disparagingly about the Irish and doubted they would take the threat to their economy seriously, Swift wrote desperately and passionately about the need to act. He opened the first of Drapier's letters with strong words: "What I intend now to say to you, is, next to your Duty to God, and the Care of your Salvation, of the greatest Concern to your selves, and your Children." Writing in simple language that could be easily understood, Swift explained how much harm Wood's Halfpence could do if it were introduced in Ireland, and he urged that his readers reject its use: "THEREFORE, my Friends, stand to it One and All: Refuse this Filthy Trash. It is no Treason to rebel against Mr. Wood." In his closing statements, Swift noted, "if Mr. Wood's Project should take, it will ruin even our Beggars."

The words in Swift's pamphlet resonated with the public and encouraged the formation of a committee to examine the new currency. The group suggested a compromise: Wood's Halfpence would be introduced in Ireland, but in a much smaller quantity than the amount previously proposed. Swift refused to negotiate on the issue. A second letter from M. B. Drapier followed the first:

> Let Mr. Wood and his Crew of Founders and Tinkers coin on till there is not an old Kettle left in the Kingdom: Let them coin old Leather, Tobacco-pipe Clay, or the Dirt in the Streets. . . . we are not under any Concern to know how he and his Tribe or Accomplices think fit to employ themselves. But I hope, and trust, that we are all to a Man fully determined to have nothing to do with him or his Ware.

This letter was published in the newspaper that first reported the proposed compromise.

Swift was just getting started. From 1724 until the summer of 1725, he wrote seven *Drapier's Letters*, along with several related pieces and commentaries on the controversial issue. Swift had quickly realized that the battle to prevent the imposition of Wood's Halfpence on Ireland would not be won with the publication of just one or two pamphlets. He also recognized that the issue was not only about a new currency that would harm Ireland's economy. The halfpence controversy allowed him to bring people's attention to Ireland's many grievances, resulting from the country's colonial relationship with Britain.

The third and fourth letters, *Some Observations* and *To the Whole People of Ireland*, cried out for the rights of the Irish people, and for their liberation from an unjust double standard. "WERE not the People of Ireland born as free as those of England?" Swift asked indignantly in the third

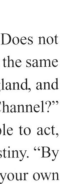

letter. "Are they not Subjects of the same King? Does not the same Sun shine over them? And have they not the same God for their Protector? Am I a Free-man in England, and do I become a Slave in six Hours, by crossing the Channel?" The fourth letter also called upon the Irish people to act, demanding that they take control of their own destiny. "By the Laws of GOD, of NATURE, of NATIONS, and of your own Country, you ARE and OUGHT to be as FREE a People as your Brethren in England," Swift insisted. While he acknowledged that the people of Ireland were under England's rule, he concluded that because they had their own separate parliament, they also had the right to make decisions regarding their nation.

Swift's powerful arguments in *The Drapier's Letters* gained him many friends and also many enemies. By now, he was getting used to bailing printers who had produced his works out of jail. However, he could not help John Harding, the printer of *The Drapier's Letters*, in time. Harding died in prison.

Swift was also faced with a familiar problem: whether it was possible to keep his old friends and still maintain his political convictions. In 1724, John Carteret, whom Swift had known in London, had been appointed the new Lord Lieutenant of Ireland. Swift believed that Carteret might agree with the opposition to Wood's Halfpence. He even sent a copy of the first *Drapier's Letter* to Carteret, accompanied by a letter stating, "When your Excellency shall be thoroughly informed, your justice and compassion for an injured people will force you to employ your credit for their relief."

After a few weeks, having received no reply, Swift wrote an irritated follow-up letter. "I could have wished your Excellency had condescended so far, as to let one of your under-clerks have signified to me that a letter was received," he complained. "I know not how your own conceptions of yourself may alter, by every new high station, but mine must continue the same, or alter for the worse."

When Carteret wrote back, he apologized for the delay in responding to Swift, explaining that he had been out of the country. However, Carteret would not commit himself regarding the topic of the pamphlet, saying, "The principal affaire You mention is under examination, & till that is over, I am not inform'd sufficiently to make any other judgement of the matter."

But Carteret also had to do his duty as Lord Lieutenant, at least in public. After the appearance of the fourth *Drapier's Letter*, Carteret called the piece treasonous. He offered a reward of three hundred British pounds to anyone who could identify the author of the pamphlets, although he must have known that it was Swift. Meanwhile, as Swift continued to fire out more pamphlets, Carteret quietly made moves toward the cancellation of Wood's Halfpence.

Ultimately, Swift's political pressure worked. In August 1725, the English government decided to cancel the halfpence. When Swift heard the news, he stopped the publication of the latest pamphlet, explaining in a letter to his friend Reverend John Worrall, "The work is done, and there is no more need of the Drapier."

Just as Swift was being celebrated as a great Irish hero

who had rallied the Irish people to successfully oppose British oppression, he left Dublin for a visit with the Sheridans. Two months later a bishop in Dublin reported that Swift was still being celebrated as a hero. "That Writer," he wrote, "is, at present, in great Repute; the Darling of the populace; His Image and Superscription on a great many Sign-Posts in this City and other great Towns." After the Drapier episode, the people of Dublin began to celebrate Swift's birthday annually by setting festive bonfires and shooting off cannons.

With the publication of *The Drapier's Letters*, Swift had created something greater than himself. The introduction of Wood's Halfpence into the Irish economy might have gone ahead if Swift had not thrown his extraordinary talent behind the campaign to prevent its use. The success of *The Drapier's Letters* showed Swift that he could accomplish much good and gain an audience for his work outside of England. He decided to continue writing political pamphlets on behalf of the Irish people.

In March 1726, Swift traveled to England for the first time in twelve years. The early part of his visit rekindled happy memories as he spent time with old friends, especially fellow members of the Scriblerus Club, including Alexander Pope and John Arbuthnot. Swift wrote to Knightley Chetwode of his reasons for visiting England. "Mine were onely to see some old Friends before my Death, and some other little Affairs that related to Summer," he explained.

The English political establishment also hoped to

Although the term was never used in his lifetime, Sir Robert Walpole is considered the first prime minister of Britain. His influence grew over the reigns of two monarchs, until he became the uncontested leader of Parliament. Some believe that his Licensing Act of 1737, which determined that all plays must be approved by a government official, was a direct attack on Swift and his literary friends. (Courtesy of the National Portrait Gallery.)

benefit from Swift's genius. Sir Robert Walpole, a Whig politician who held several key governmental posts under King George I, met with Swift to discuss the political and economic condition of Ireland. In his letter to Chetwode, Swift declared that his intention was only "to represent the affairs of Ireland to him in a true light." However, he and Walpole did not see eye to eye, he explained. "Sir Robert Walpole was pleased to enlarge very much upon the subject of Ireland, in a manner so alien from what I conceived to be rights and privileges of a subject of England, that I did not think proper to debate the matter with him as much as I otherwise might," he reported, "because I found it would be in vain."

After the unsuccessful meeting with Walpole, Swift received bad news. Stella had been very ill for some time. Now, his friends in Ireland sent word that she was getting worse. In July, he wrote to Sheridan. "I look upon this to be the greatest Event that can ever happen to me, but all my Preparations will not suffice to make me bear it like a Philosopher, nor altogether like a Christian. There hath been the most intimate Friendship between us from her Childhood."

Five months after his arrival in England, Swift decided to go back to Ireland. But before leaving London in August 1726, Swift arranged for the publication of a book that he had been working on for almost six years—*Gulliver's Travels*. Many of his literary friends knew Swift had been working on a lengthy manuscript. Alexander Pope had referred to it a year earlier in a letter to Swift, noting "Your Travels I hear much of." Soon many more people would be hearing of *Gulliver's Travels*.

CHAPTER SEVEN

Gulliver

By October 1726, when *Gulliver's Travels* was published, few people disputed Jonathan Swift's writing talent or his passion for the causes he adopted. As a clergyman, he had not achieved the recognition and the high position that he had sought. But few of his contemporaries, especially in Ireland, would have called him a failure. With his Irish political tracts, and especially *The Drapier's Letters*, Swift had helped change Irish history—an achievement that would make him one of the most famous Irishmen of all time. *Gulliver's Travels*, published quite late in his life, would eventually make him beloved of centuries of readers. Because of its imaginative story line and simply written prose, it would even become a classic for children.

Although *Gulliver's Travels* was published anonymously, most people knew its author was Jonathan Swift. It was an immediate success. One month after its publication, Swift's friends John Gay and Alexander Pope wrote to tell him that it was being read and enjoyed "from the cabinet-council to the nursery." Soon afterward Pope wrote again to congratulate the author and added, "I prophecy [*Gulliver's Travels*] will be in future the admiration of all men."

Swift was delighted to learn that some people totally misunderstood the book, believing it to be an actual travelogue)) that described real places. Unaware that the book was satire, these confused readers questioned its truthfulness. In a letter to his friend Pope, Swift noted, "A Bishop here said, that book was full of improbable lies, and for his part, he hardly believed a word of it."

While Swift was working on *Gulliver's Travels*, he read many travel books, which gave detailed descriptions of journeys through lands both close to home and in unfamiliar countries and cultures. In his own work, he parodied these publications. When the book was first published, Swift entitled it *Travels into Several Remote Nations of the World, in Four Parts.*

Even though the book's content should have made it obvious that *Gulliver's Travels* was a work of fiction, Swift presented it as a factual story. Captain Lemuel Gulliver is listed as the author, and a portrait of him appears in the front of the book. The beginning also features a letter written by Captain Gulliver to his cousin Richard Sympson, another fictional character who supposedly edited the manuscript.

In the letter, Gulliver refers irritably to the poor quality of Sympson's editing. "I do not remember I gave you Power

In an effort to protect himself from prosecution, Swift's publisher Benjamin Mott changed, omitted, and added to several parts of Gulliver's Travels. *When it was reprinted in 1735, Swift returned the manuscript to its intended form and added the letter from Gulliver to his cousin to retain authenticity and explain the changes between the two editions.* (University of Leeds, United Kingdom)

to consent, that any thing should be omitted," he complains, "and much less that any thing should be inserted." Swift also included a foreword written by Sympson that is entitled "The Publisher to the Reader." In it, he guiltily admits, "I have Reason to apprehend that Mr. *Gulliver* may be a little dissatisfied."

In the opening lines of *Gulliver's Travels*, the fictional narrator, Gulliver, describes his family background, his education, and how he came to go to sea. Swift uses this narrator, whose sometimes simple-minded comments differ from the observations and interpretations of the reader, as a way to introduce irony into the book.

In his journeys, Gulliver travels to several fictional countries. They include the imaginary lands of Lilliput, Blefuscu, Brobdingnag, Laputa, and the land of the Houyhnhnms. However, the country that most readers remember is Lilliput, the first place that Gulliver visits.

After his ship is wrecked near the island of Lilliput, Gulliver manages to swim ashore and then falls into a deep sleep from exhaustion. Later, he wakes to find himself firmly tied to the ground and being closely examined by "a human Creature not six Inches high." Although he becomes the prisoner of the tiny people, called Lilliputians, Gulliver "gains Favour by his mild Disposition," and eventually helps to defend them in their war with the people of Blefescu. Gulliver explains how the war between the two nations broke out because their leaders disagreed about how cooked eggs should be opened:

> It is allowed on all Hands, that the primitive Way of breaking Eggs before we eat them, was upon the larger End: But his present Majesty's Grand-father, while he was a Boy, going to eat an Egg, and breaking it according to the ancient Practice, happened to cut one of his Fingers. Whereupon the Emperor, his Father, published an Edict, commanding all his Subjects, upon great Penalties, to break the smaller End of their Eggs. . . . [C]ivil Commotions [caused by this law] were constantly fomented by the Monarchs of Blefescu; and when they were quelled, the Exiles always fled for Refuge to that Empire.

In this first section of the book, Swift deftly satirizes

politics in society. He makes his point clear: many wars and political conflicts are caused by small, often trivial, differences.

Swift uses Gulliver's great size, compared to that of the tiny Lilliputians, to show symbolically that his moral stature is much greater than theirs. In the same way, in the next voyage, the author portrays Gulliver as belonging to the less moral race, in comparison to the giant inhabitants of Brobdingnag. When Gulliver tries to impress

Swift's map indicates that Brobdingnag is located in northern California on a peninsula separated from the rest of the land by large volcanoes. Gulliver's first acquaintance in Brobdingnag was less scrupulous than his king. In fact, as this picture depicts, the farmer exhibited him as a curiosity and collected a great deal of money from his neighbors and countrymen. (Courtesy of Art Resource.)

Brobdingnag's king by describing his country's history, the king is horrified by the account. The history of Gulliver's people, the king insists, is "only an Heap of Conspiracies, Rebellions, Murders, Massacres, Revolutions, [and] Banishments." He eventually concludes that Gulliver's fellow humans are "the most pernicious Race of little odious Vermin that Nature ever suffered to crawl upon the Surface of the Earth."

On his third voyage, to the nation of Laputa, Gulliver visits the Academy of Lagado, an institute of learning. In this section of the book, Swift mocks the extreme ideas of some philosophers and scientists. One professor at the academy "had been Eight Years upon a Project for extracting Sun-Beams out of Cucumbers," Gulliver reports. Another professor experiments cruelly with a dog and kills it. These strange experiments recall the efforts of some members of the Dublin Philosophical Society, with which Swift was familiar during his schooling at Trinity College in Dublin.

Gulliver's fourth journey, to the land of the Houyhnhnms (pronounced WIN-ums) and the Yahoos, contains some of the most savagely bitter satire that Swift ever wrote. The Houyhnhnms are a race of highly civilized talking horses, and the Yahoos are barbaric creatures, resembling humans but without reason and conscience. (The word *yahoo,* meaning a very badly behaved person, has since passed into the English language.) After spending time among the Houyhnhnms, Gulliver decides that they, rather than humans, are the rational animals. When he returns to England,

Houyhnhnms, who are dignified and reasonable far beyond both humanity and the perverse Yahoos, call themselves "the perfection of nature." Many literary critics deeply dislike these superior horses, even saying that the writing of this section is proof of Swift's deteriorating mental condition. (Courtsey of Art Resource.)

he rejects his family and denounces mankind, preferring to spend his time with his horses.

Gulliver's Travels sums up many of the main concerns of Swift's career. The book reveals his talent for telling a good story to prove a point. At the same time, *Gulliver's*

Travels is sometimes shockingly bitter. Its negative comments on the nature of mankind culminate in a conclusion that does not offer much hope for the human race. At the end of the book, Gulliver believes that he has only two choices. He can return to what he now regards as the life of a Yahoo, or he can turn away in disgust from his fellow humans and be judged insane.

Some people believe that the conclusion of *Gulliver's Travels* demonstrates that the book's author had a deep hatred for human beings. However, it is clear from the many relationships and friendships that Jonathan Swift maintained throughout his lifetime that he did not regard all people as Yahoos. Although often cynical about human behavior and the progress of history in general, Swift saw some good in humanity. Through his use of satire, *Gulliver's Travels* allowed him not only to mock the foolish things that people do, but also to point out the faults in human nature with the hope of improving it. As with his writing and political campaigning, he hoped that the satire of his book might unsettle the complacency of the reader and bring about change for the better.

About six months after the publication of *Gulliver's Travels,* in April of 1727, Swift traveled to England once more. Now fifty-nine years old, he knew that his visit was likely to be his last, and he made a point of visiting places that had been important to him and his family. On the way to London, he stopped by the Swift family home in Herefordshire, and saw the church where his grandfather had preached. He also went to Oxford, where he visited friends and relatives of his friend Robert Harley, who had died in 1724.

In London, Swift stayed with his friend Alexander Pope. There he found that the Whig government viewed his presence with suspicion, while the Tories wanted him to get involved in their political campaigns. "You will wonder to find me say so much of Politicks," he wrote to Thomas Sheridan back in Ireland, "but I keep very bad Company, who are full of nothing else."

Swift considered traveling on to France. Such a journey would have been his first and only time away from the British Isles. However, King George I died in June 1727. As political questions arose over who would succeed him, Swift abandoned his plans to travel to France and stayed in England, where he considered whether he should go back into political life.

That summer Swift received reports from friends in Ireland that Stella was very ill. Instead of rushing back to be by her side, he remained in London for a while, undecided about whether to return to Ireland to be with Stella, or to stay in England and avoid witnessing the end of her life. "I do not intend to return to Ireland so soon as I purposed; I would not be there in the very midst of Grief," he wrote sadly to Sheridan that August. A few days later, in another letter to Sheridan, he observed, "The last Act of Life is always a Tragedy at best; but it is a bitter Aggravation to have one's best Friend go before one."

Swift's own problem with vertigo, which had grown much worse in recent years, added to his misery. Finally,

Holyhead has been a destination for travel between the United Kingdom and Ireland since prehistoric times. Swift is one among many who have had to wait in that beautiful but inhospitable place for fair sailing weather. (Library of Congress)

in late September he left London. But then he was delayed at Holyhead, on the windswept Welsh island of Anglesey. It was his usual crossing place between Britain and Ireland, but for several days the wind did not blow in the right direction to take his ship across the Irish Sea.

To pass the time, Swift kept a journal of his thoughts, a daily account that was later published as *Holyhead Journal.* In the *Journal,* he recorded his feelings. "Here I could live with two or three friends in a warm house, and good wine—much better than being a Slave in Ireld," he complained, before listing his woes. "But my misery is, that I am in the worst part of wales under the very worst circumstances; afraid of a relapse; in utmost solitude; impatient for the condition of our friend; not a soul to converse with, hinderd from exercise by rain, cooped up in a room not half so large as one of the Deanry Closets."

Stella was still alive when Swift returned to Ireland, although she lived for only a few more months. She died on January 28, 1728, at the age of forty-six. Upon receiving news of her death, Swift immediately began to write a short biography about her as a way to express his sadness and feelings of loss. However, he could not complete his work that night. A poignant note in the piece, later published as "On the Death of Mrs. Johnson," reads, "My Head achs, and I can write no more."

Swift did not attend his good friend's funeral. His own ill health and the depth of his mourning forced him to stay at home. However, he later finished the biographical sketch of Stella's life, stating, "She had indeed reason to love a country [Ireland], where she had the esteem and friendship of all who knew her, and the universal good report of all who ever heard of her."

Swift had experienced many relationships in the course of his life. Some friendships had failed because of political differences. In the case of Vanessa Van Homrigh, differing expectations about their relationship resulted in a bitter end to that friendship. In contrast, Swift's friendship with Stella Johnson remained constant. It lasted for forty years, ending only with her death. Swift considered his relationship with Stella as one of the most precious experiences of his life.

Swift's close friends must have understood his grief over Stella's death, even though they did not mention it directly.

Two weeks later, a kind letter from Alexander Pope showed his concern for his friend. "I hear that you have had some return of your illness which carried you so suddenly from us (if indeed it was your own illness which made you in such haste to be at Dublin)," Pope wrote. "Dear Swift take care of your health."

In the years following Stella's death, Swift kept himself busy in Ireland. His poor health would not allow him to take any more trips to England, but at this point in his life he had accepted Ireland as his home. Still, he missed his English friends, such as Pope, who like Swift was prohibited from traveling because of poor health. In a letter to Pope he acknowledged that both of them were where they belonged: "God forbid I should condemn you to Ireland . . . and for England I despair; and indeed a change of affairs would come too late at my season of life, and might probably produce nothing on my behalf."

Sometime during the late 1720s, Swift started to write his autobiography, which he called *Family of Swift*. He never completed the work, however, and it ran to just a few pages. Swift preferred to spend time on another writing project, one that allowed him to work with his good friend Thomas Sheridan. In May 1728, Swift and Sheridan started a new paper in Dublin. Called *The Intelligencer*, the publication featured stories written by both men. Swift wrote an essay defending John Gay's controversial *Beggar's Opera*, a satiric play that lampooned the Whig statesman Robert Walpole. The play, first produced that year, had been hugely successful in London, despite its potentially dangerous political satire.

Swift's essays for *The Intelligencer* were sometimes political, but the paper did not really support the Whigs or the Tories. In one pamphlet reprinted in *The Intelligencer*, Swift returned to some of the subjects that he had addressed in *The Drapier's Letters*. His essay *A Short View of the State of Ireland* mocked the position held by some British government officials that Ireland was thriving socially and economically. "There is not one Argument used to prove the Riches of Ireland, which is not a logical Demonstration of its Poverty," Swift told his readers. He concluded his argument by stating, "If Ireland be a rich and flourishing Kingdom; its Wealth and Prosperity must be owing to certain Causes, that are yet concealed from the whole Race of Mankind; and the Effects are equally invisible."

Disturbed by the continuing unjust economic exploitation of Ireland by Great Britain, Swift could not restrain his anger and agitation. Alexander Pope wrote to his friend sympathetically, "I truly share in all that troubles you, and wish you remov'd from a scene of distress, which I know works your compassionate temper too strongly."

Ireland's wretched poverty moved Swift to write *A Modest Proposal* in 1729. His satiric pamphlet about eating Irish babies and using their skins as leather is horrifying because of its concept of cannibalism. But the political tract is also disturbing because of the casual tone of its narrator, who cites statistics to support his proposal and compares the practicality of his baby-eating scheme to other projects that had failed to help the Irish.

Swift did not intend that readers take *A Modest Proposal* seriously. He was making use of irony. His purpose in writing *A Modest Proposal* was to bring about change that would save Irish babies from starvation, not have them killed. His extreme "solution" was intended to shock both the Irish and the English into making some changes for the good of Ireland.

Although Swift would remain pessimistic about Ireland's future prospects, he did see improvements in the country during his lifetime. The city of Dublin continued to grow, and with growth came more jobs. Many of the city's most stately buildings, including the Parliament House, were built during the 1720s and 1730s. However, Swift was

The Liffey River flows though the center of Dublin, dividing it into halves. The Four Courts, which held the law courts of Ireland, can be seen on the right. This impressive building was destroyed in 1922, effectively erasing more than 1,000 years of history housed in the records room beneath it. (British Library)

The building on this hilltop about a mile from Dublin is a powder magazine, a place to guard weapons from theft and protect gunpowder from fire. When it was built in 1738, Swift poked fun at the project, wittily remarking, "Behold the proof of Irish sense, here Irish wit is seen: When nothing's left that's worth defense, we build a magazine." (British Library)

well aware that the Irish parliament, which met at the Parliament House, was controlled by Great Britain.

Jonathan Swift wrote other pamphlets on political and religious subjects during the 1730s. In the last decade of his literary life, the elderly dean turned to poetry, writing mostly on the subjects of politics, friendship, and women.

When he was more than seventy years old, Swift wrote one of his best-known poems, called "Verses on the Death of Dr. Swift." In this work, Swift confronts the reality of his own impending death, while also looking back on the accomplishments of his life. He reflects on the feebleness brought on by old age and how his younger friends will congratulate themselves for not being in such dire condition as Swift. According to the poem, his friends would "hug themselves, and reason thus; / 'It is not yet so bad with us.'"

Upon his death, Swift said, his friends would react with different degrees of sorrow: "Poor Pope will grieve a month; and Gay / A week; and Arbuthnot a day." In the poem, Swift also acknowledges that during his lifetime, he may have been too harsh in his writing. However, the issues of the time had required such indignation:

> Perhaps I may allow the Dean
> Had too much satire in his vein;
> And seemed determined not to starve it,
> Because no age could more deserve it.

Swift acknowledges that some people would probably not grieve when he died. But others would celebrate the accomplishments of his life, particularly his efforts to help the Irish people obtain their rights under British rule.

> He never courted men in station,
> Nor persons had in admiration;
> Of no man's greatness was afraid,
> Because he sought for no man's aid.

> . . .

> Fair LIBERTY was all his cry;
> For her he stood prepared to die;
> For her he boldly stood alone;
> For her he oft exposed his own.

As it turned out, Swift actually lived longer than most of his closest friends. Many of his literary contemporaries died during the 1730s. In December 1732, Alexander Pope and John Arbuthnot sent a letter with the news of John Gay's death. When Swift received the note, he did not open it for five days because of "an impulse foreboding some misfortune." Three years later, in February 1735, Arbuthnot also died.

Many of the letters Swift wrote during the 1730s to friends in England and Ireland mention his declining health. In 1736, he wrote to Thomas Sheridan, who was also ill, with his usual combination of a little self-pity and a good deal of black humor. "My Head is ever bad; and I have just as much Spirits left as a drowned Mouse," he grumbled. "What you say of your Leanness is incredible. . . . But if you continue to breathe free, (which nothing but Exercise can give) you may be safe with as little Flesh as I, which is none at all."

Although many years younger than Swift, Sheridan died before him, in 1738. Swift would elude death for several more years, but toward the end of his life, ill health would affect not only his body but also his powerful mind.

CHAPTER EIGHT

"Swift Has Sailed into His Rest"

Jonathan Swift continued to live an active life well into his early seventies. He passed his time taking horseback rides, an activity he had always enjoyed, although he had to be careful to avoid falls. He also continued to attend to his duties, to the best of his ability, as dean of St. Patrick's Cathedral. But Menière's disease had caused a profound hearing loss that increasingly isolated him from others. Swift described his feelings of physical and mental loneliness in a short, sad poem entitled "On His Own Deafness."

Despite his own health problems, Swift expressed concern for the well-being of others. When he heard of the illness of Mrs. Whiteway, a cousin who since the mid-1730s had helped to look after him and the Deanery, he sent her an anxious letter. "Your son . . . gave me a very melancholy account of your ill health, extremely to my grief," he wrote.

"I am in very great pain about you; for the weather is so extremely sharp, that it must needs add to your disorders."

In 1740, at the age of seventy-two, Swift suffered a stroke that caused memory loss and aphasia (difficulty producing and understanding speech). In May of that year, after Swift received a letter from Alexander Pope but did not answer it, Mrs. Whiteway wrote to Pope herself to explain his situation. "I take the liberty to tell you (with grief of heart) his memory is so much impaired, that in a few hours he forgot [the letter]," she apologized.

Around this time, Swift drew up his will. It included presents and legacies to friends and clergymen in both Ireland and England. However, Swift designated that almost all of his fortune be used to establish a mental hospital in or near Dublin. As dean of St. Patrick's, Swift had seen how people with mental illnesses were neglected and abused. He decided that upon his death, his estate would go toward the construction of an institution that would protect and treat these unfortunate people.

In June 1742, Swift had a public dispute with his friend Francis Wilson, a young clergyman who had frequently visited him at the St. Patrick's Deanery. One evening Wilson invited Swift back to his house in Clondalkin, a village south of Dublin. There, he tried to get Swift drunk. Swift's cousin, Deane Swift, accompanied the two men in the coach on their way back to Dublin. According to Deane Swift, "Wilson began to grow very noisy, and to curse and swear, and to abuse the Dean [Swift] most horribly. . . . Whether he struck the Dean

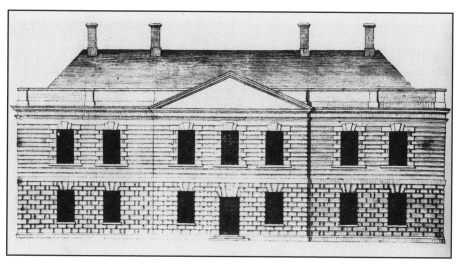

St. Patrick's Hospital was the first mental hospital in Ireland. Swift's detailed plans and his ideas about the treatment of the mentally ill have been followed since the hospital was founded in 1757. The hospital still functions today. (National Library of Ireland)

or not is uncertain, but, one of the Dean's arms was observed, next morning, to be black and blue." However, others said that Swift had started the fight, not Wilson.

In any case, it had become clear that Swift's mental health was failing. That year a Commission of Lunacy was appointed to examine his mental condition. The members of the Commission declared that the dean was of unsound mind and placed him and his estate under the care of guardians.

During the last few years of his life, Swift was looked after by servants and visited by relatives, but he could not properly communicate or make himself understood. It was a tragic prelude to his death; the man who had always expressed himself so clearly and forcefully was reduced to incoherence. Deane Swift described the elderly man's struggles to make himself understood. "He shrugged his shoulders, and, rocking himself, said, I am what I am, I am what I am," Swift's cousin wrote. "He endeavoured several times to speak to his servant . . . at last, not finding words to express what he would be at, after some uneasiness, he said 'I am a fool.'"

On October 19, 1745, Jonathan Swift died at the age of seventy-eight. He lay in state for three days at the Deanery. During that time, crowds of people came to pay their respects to the renowned Anglo-Irishman. Reportedly, some of them also stole pieces of his hair as souvenirs. His friend Pope had died only a year before, leaving Swift as one of the last representatives of a great literary generation.

In 1755, Jonathan Swift's first biographer, a great-nephew named Deane Swift, published the autobiographical fragment *Family of Swift,* which had been written almost thirty years earlier. Swift's letters to Stella, written from 1710 to 1713, were also published posthumously, some in 1766 and the remainder in 1768. Through his books, pamphlets, and poems, Jonathan Swift is still remembered in Ireland, and especially Dublin. His works continue to inspire and amuse, and they remain his most famous legacy.

Swift is remembered in Dublin in other ways as well. As he had requested in his will, most of his fortune was used to establish a hospital for the mentally ill. Designed by the architect George Semple, St. Patrick's Hospital opened its doors in 1757. Also referred to as Swift's Hospital, it is the oldest psychiatric hospital still operating on its original site in the British Isles today.

Although he was born of English parents and raised an

Anglican in a Catholic country, Jonathan Swift is considered by the Irish people to be one of their own. Centuries after his death they continue to honor Swift in recognition of his service to the Irish people. Because he passionately attacked the causes of Irish poverty and oppression in his writings, Swift changed the thinking of the world around him.

Recognizing Swift's place in the nation's history, Ireland has featured the author's image on both its postage and currency. In 1967, the Republic of Ireland celebrated the tercentenary of Jonathan Swift's birth by issuing a postage stamp in his honor. It showed a bust of the author, placed before the arched windows of St. Patrick's Cathedral, where he served so many years as dean. During the late 1970s, the Central Bank of Ireland issued a purple, ten-pound bank

Ireland has not forgotten Swift, one of its staunchest champions.

note with Swift's portrait. A map of eighteenth-century Dublin illustrated the reverse side of the bank note. The currency remained in circulation in Ireland until 2001.

St. Patrick's Cathedral is also the site of Swift's grave, which is located in the southwestern corner of the great cathedral, next to Stella's. Various memorials and items commemorating Swift's life can also be found there. They include the bust depicted on the 1967 postage stamp, a selection of Swift's writings, and his death mask (a plaster mold of his face made shortly after his death). Other Swift memorabilia include a document awarding him the Freedom of the City of Dublin and the pulpit from which he preached.

Swift wrote his own epitaph, in Latin. It is carved, with gold letters, into a black marble slab that hangs in St. Patrick's Cathedral on the wall above his grave. The epitaph's best-known English translation appeared almost two hundred years later, written by William Butler Yeats, the great Anglo-Irish poet who deeply admired Swift and his power of words:

> Swift has sailed into his rest;
> Savage indignation there
> Cannot lacerate his breast.
> Imitate him, if you dare,
> World-besotted traveller; he
> Served human liberty.

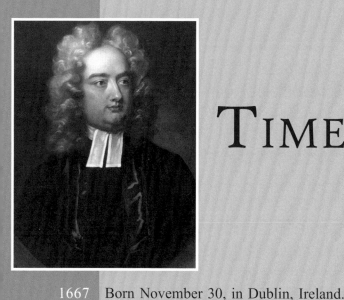

TIMELINE

1667   Born November 30, in Dublin, Ireland.

1669   By his own account, is taken by his nurse to England for three years.

1673   Attends Kilkenny College, near Dublin, through 1682.

1682   Enters Trinity College, Dublin.

1686   Graduates with a bachelor of arts degree from Trinity College.

1689   Goes to live at Moor Park, Surrey, with Sir William Temple and his household; meets Esther Johnson, whom he calls Stella.

1690   First symptoms of Menière's disease appear; returns to Ireland during political turmoil as the forces of King William defeat James II at the Battle of the Boyne.

1691   Returns to Moor Park and begins writing in earnest.

1692   Graduates with a master of arts degree from Hart Hall, at the University of Oxford; publishes first poem.

1694   Returns to Dublin, Ireland, where he is ordained as a clergyman.

1695   Goes to live in the parish of Kilroot, in northern Ireland.

1696   After his marriage proposal to Jane Waring is rejected, returns to Moor Park.

1699	Sir William Temple dies. Returns to Dublin as chaplain and secretary to Earl of Berkeley.
1700	Appointed to position of vicar at parish of Laracor, near Dublin; also assumes Prebend of Dunlavin at St. Patrick's Cathedral.
1701	Awarded doctor of divinity from Dublin University; visits England, where he publishes his first political pamphlet, *A Discourse of the Contests and Dissensions between the Nobles and the Commons in Athens and Rome.* Stella Johnson and Rebecca Dingley move to Ireland.
1703	Returns to London for the opening of Parliament, and stays for six months.
1704	Publishes *A Tale of a Tub* and *Battle of the Books* anonymously.
1707	Sent to England for two years on a mission requesting Queen Anne to eliminate First Fruits tax being levied on the Church of Ireland; meets Esther Van Homrigh, whom he refers to as Vanessa; enters London literary circles and publishes *Bickerstaff Papers.*
1710	Mother, Abigail Errick, dies; after Tory government assumes power, Swift joins the Tory Party and serves as editor of its publication, *Examiner*; begins writing detailed letters to Stella about London life, later published as *Journal to Stella.*
1711	Publishes *The Conduct of the Allies.*
1713	Returns to Dublin to take up position of dean of St. Patrick's, but returns to London in September.
1714	Publishes *The Public Spirit of the Whigs*; starts Scriblerus Club with other writers, including Alexander Pope and John Arbuthnot; after the death of Queen Anne on August 1, returns to Dublin.
1717	Preaches sermon *On Brotherly Love* in St. Patrick's Cathedral.

1718	Befriends Irish writers Thomas Sheridan and Patrick Delany.
1720	After collapse of English government's South Sea Company initiative, publishes *A Proposal for the Universal Use of Irish Manufacture*.
1723	Death of Vanessa.
1724	Controversy in Ireland over proposed introduction of Wood's Halfpence inspires Swift to publish seven *Drapier's Letters* and related pieces condemning the cheap currency; Swift is hailed as hero when coinage is canceled.
1726	Visits England for the first time in twelve years; publishes *Gulliver's Travels*.
1727	Makes final visit to England. After death of George I, returns to Dublin.
1728	Death of Stella in January; produces *The Intelligencer* with Sheridan.
1729	Publishes *A Modest Proposal*.
1731	Writes poem "Verses on the Death of Dr Swift."
1735	Publication of Swift's *Works,* a collection of his writings.
1742	Requires care by guardians after being declared to be of unsound mind.
1745	Dies on October 19 and is buried in St. Patrick's Cathedral, alongside Stella.
1757	St. Patrick's Hospital, also referred to as Swift's Hospital because of his endowment, opens its doors.

SOURCES

CHAPTER ONE: Dubliner

p. 12, "I have been assured . . . for fine Gentlemen." Jonathan Swift, *The Prose Writings of Jonathan Swift,* (Oxford: Basil Blackwell, 1968), vol. 12, 111–112.

p. 12, I GRANT this Food . . . " Ibid.,112.

p. 14, "wonderfully mend the World," A. Norman Jeffares, ed. *Fair Liberty Was All His Cry: A Tercentenary Tribute to Jonathan Swift, 1667–1745* (London: Macmillan, 1967), 12.

p. 16, "ten Sons and three . . . " Swift, *Prose Writings,* vol. 5, 190.

p. 17, "of all mortals . . . " David Nokes, *Jonathan Swift: A Hypocrite Reversed* (Oxford: Oxford University Press, 1985), 7.

p. 17, "on both sides very indiscreet . . ." Swift, *Prose Writings,* vol. 5, 192.

p. 17, "extremely fond of the infant," Ibid., 192.

p. 17, "For when the matter . . ." Ibid., 192.

p. 19, "I formerly used to envy . . ." David Woolley, ed. *The Correspondence of Jonathan Swift* (Frankfurt: Peter Lang GmbH, 1999), vol. 1, 217.

p. 20, "the education of a dog," A. L. Rowse, *Jonathan Swift: Major Prophet* (London: Thames and Hudson, 1975), 13.

p. 20, "by the ill Treatment . . ." Swift, *Prose Writings,* vol. 5, 192.

p. 21, "I was quickly weary . . ." Irvin Ehrenpreis, *Swift: The Man, His Works, and the Age* (London: Methuen & Co Ltd, 1983), vol. 1, 48.

p. 21-22, "It has been affirmed . . ." Swift, *Prose Writings*, vol. 5, 211.

p. 23, "very regular discourses concerning . . ." Ehrenpreis, *Swift: The Man, His Works, and the Age*, vol. 1, 80.

p. 25, "lived with great Regularity . . ." Swift, *Prose Writings*, vol. 5, 192.

p. 25, "neglect of duties . . ." Ehrenpreis, *Swift: The Man, His Works, and the Age*, vol. 1, 69.

p. 25, "he was stopped of . . ." Swift, *Prose Writings*, vol. 5, 192.

CHAPTER TWO: Moor Park

p. 33, "had been a great Friend . . ." Swift, *Prose Writings*, vol. 5, 193.

p. 33-34, "both a great . . ." Bruce Arnold, *Swift: An Illustrated Life* (Dublin: Lilliput Press, 1999), 32.

p. 34, "His whole family having . . ." Woolley, *Correspondence*, vol. 1, 101.

p. 35, "a man of virtue," Swift, *Prose Writings*, vol. 5, 276.

p. 36, "He returned to Ireld . . ." Ibid., 193.

p. 37, "I . . . had some share . . ." Ibid., 227.

p. 38, "In these seven weeks . . ." Woolley, *Correspondence*, vol. 1, 104.

p. 39, "Shall I believe . . ." Jonathan Swift, *The Complete Poems* (London: Yale University Press, 1983), 59.

p. 39, "This was the first time . . ." Swift, *Prose Writings*, vol. 5, 194.

p. 39, "Tho' he promises . . ." Woolley, *Correspondence,* vol. 1, 116.

p. 40, "He was extream angry . . ." Woolley, *Correspondence*, vol. 1, 120.

p. 40-41, "That I might not continue . . ." Ibid., 122.

CHAPTER THREE: "For the Universal Improvement of Mankind"

p. 44, "The inhabitants (except my family . . ." Ehrenpreis, *Swift: The Man, His Works, and the Age*, 160.

p. 45, "having never entertained . . ." Woolley, *Correspondence*, vol. 1, 136.

p. 46, "How far you will stretch . . ." Ibid., 125.

p. 46, "Varina's life is daily wasting . . ." Ibid., 124.

p. 46, "Only remember . . ." Ibid., 127

p. 46, "I am once more offered . . ." Ibid., 125.

p. 47, "growing weary [of Kilroot] . . ." Swift, *Prose Writings*, vol. 5, 194.

p. 48, "Once upon a Time . . ." Swift, *Prose Writings*, vol. 1, 44.

p. 49, "A person that feared . . ." Ibid., 125.

p. 49-50, "They [Calvinists] quarrel . . ." Ibid., 125.

p. 50, "resolving in no Case . . ." Ibid., 85.

p. 50, "a True Critick . . ." Ibid., 58.

p. 50, "I am now trying . . ." Ibid., 133.

p. 51, "a sort of Glass . . ." Ibid., xx.

p. 51, "a person of the greatest . . ." Ehrenpreis, *Swift: The Man, His Works, and the Age*, 257.

p. 52-53, "Not to marry . . . I should observe none." Swift, *Prose Writings*, vol. I, xxxvii.

p. 53, "another Person had so far . . ." Ibid., vol. 5, 195.

p. 54, "The Excuse pretended was . . ." Ibid., 195.

p. 55, "The dismal account you say . . ." Woolley, *Correspondence*, vol. 1, 141.

p. 55, "Will you be ready . . ." Ibid., 142.

p. 55, "I singled you out . . ." Ibid., 143.

CHAPTER FOUR: Whigs, Tories, and Ladies

p. 60, "Then for the Irish legs . . ." Woolley, *Correspondence*, vol. 1, 149

p. 60, "[W]ho that hath a spirit . . ." Ibid., 151.

p. 61, "I found myself much inclined . . ." Swift, *Prose Writings*, vol. 8, 120.

p. 61, "I am much . . ." Ibid., 147.

p. 63, "If my fortunes. . ." Ibid., 153.

p. 64, "whether Jonathan be married? . . ." Ibid., 163.

p. 64, "If I love Ireland better. . ." Ibid., 161.

p. 67, "I have been above . . ." Ibid., 173.

p. 68, "I beg you will endeavour . . ." Ibid., 185.

p. 69, "the most Agreeable Companion . . ." A. Norman Jeffares, *Jonathan Swift* (Harhew, UK: Longman Group Ltd, 1976), 11.

p. 70, "but a Trifle . . ." Swift, *Prose Writings*, vol. 2, 145.

p. 70-71, "I dont doubt but . . ." Woolley, *Correspondence*, vol. 1, 189–190.

p. 71, "whose pleasant Writings . . ." Swift, *Prose Writings*, vol. 2, xxvi.

p. 71, "a cruel Distemper . . ." Woolley, *Correspondence*, vol. 1, 225.

p. 72, "the Proceedings in this . . ." Ibid., 248.

p. 72, "I think it is very . . ." Ibid., 259.

p. 72, "the satisfaction and Honour . . ." Ibid., 278.

p. 72, "I have now lost my barrier . . ." Swift, *Prose Writings*, vol. 5, 196.

p. 74, "would lay hold on me . . . been seen in England." Swift, *Journal to Stella* (Gloucester, UK: Alan Sutton Publishing Ltd, 1984), 5.

p. 75, "I am already represented . . ." Ibid., 19.

p. 76, "Upon shewing my commission . . ." Swift, *Prose Writings*, vol. 8, 122–123.

p. 76, "That the Queen was resolved, Ibid., 123.

p. 76, "It is a Practice . . ." Ibid., vol. 3, 3.

p. 77, "Mr Harley desired I . . ." Swift, *Journal to Stella*, 113–114.

p. 79, "And can Stella read . . ." Swift, *Journal to Stella*, 73.

p. 79, "I called at the coffeehouse . . ." Ibid., 101.

p. 79, "I am here in . . ." Ibid., 168.

p. 79, "Have I any apples . . ." Ibid., 389.

p. 80, "[The] Lord-Treasurer told . . ." Ibid., 458.

p. 80, "Perhaps I may be . . ." Ibid., 464.

p. 81, "I am condemned to live . . ." Woolley, *Correspondence*, vol. 1, 481.

p. 81, "I am riding here for . . ." Ibid., 513.

p. 81, "Neither will I leave . . ." Ibid., 513.

p. 81, "I protest I am less . . ." Ibid., 530.

CHAPTER FIVE: Literary London, Dirty Dublin

p. 82, "heartily weary of . . ." Woolley, *Correspondence*, vol. 1, 532.

p. 83, "For in your publick Capacity . . ." Ibid., 628.

p. 84-85, "The Doctor and Dean . . ." Swift, *Complete Poems*, 159–160.

p. 85, "The design of the Memoirs . . ." Nokes, *Jonathan Swift*, 203.

p. 88, "Qualities enough to denominate . . ." Swift, *Prose Writings*, vol. 8, 32.

p. 88, "What shall I say to . . ." Ibid., 36.

p. 88, "The Author of the *Crisis* . . ." Ibid., 51.

p. 88, "Whoever writes at this . . ." Ibid., 68.

p. 89, "I have heard that . . ." Woolley, *Correspondence*, vol. 1, 589.

p. 89-90, "I assure you . . ." Woolley, *Correspondence*. vol. 1, 600.

P. 90, "I am at a Clergyman's . . ." Ibid., 606.

p. 90, "I am now retired . . ." Ibid., 611.

p. 90-91, "I . . . think you . . ." Ibid., vol. 2, 44.

p. 91, "Pray don't go . . ." Ibid., 47.

p. 91, "We have certainly more heads . . ." Ibid., 58.

p. 91, "Go into Ireland . . ." Ibid., 65.

p. 91-92, "You should not have come . . . Ease of Mind. adieu."
Ibid., 71–72.

p. 92, "He now could praise, esteem . . ." Swift, *Poems*, 144.

p. 93, "I know not what to . . ." Woolley, *Correspondence*, vol.
2, 76.

p. 93, "Will you tell our Friends . . ." Ibid., 111.

p. 93, "One occasion I have . . ." Ibid., 85.

p. 93, "by her perpetual noise . . ." Ibid., 88.

p. 93-94, "You are to understand . . ." Ibid., 133.

p. 95, "there is no Duty . . ." Swift, *Prose Writings*, vol. 9, 171.

p. 95, "the Papists and Fanaticks . . ." Ibid., 172.

p. 95-96, "I would not have gone . . . the Country very
miserable." Woolley, *Correspondence*, vol. 2, 93.

p. 96, "This morning a Woman . . ." Ibid., 102.

p. 96-97, "Tis impossible to describe . . ." Ibid., 103.

p. 98, "Stella this day is . . ." Swift, *Poems*, 187.

p. 98-99, "doubtless the best . . ." Swift, *Prose Writings*, vol.
5, 216.

p. 99, "Mrs. Dingley and Mrs. Johnson . . ." Woolley, *Correspondence*, vol. 2, 312.

p. 99, "He lets his wife . . ." Swift, *Prose Writings*, vol. 5, 222.

p. 99-100, "I have long thought severall . . ." Woolley,
Correspondence, vol. 2, 279.

p. 100, "If you will recollect . . ." Ibid., 316–317.

p. 100, "The truth is. . ." Ehrenpreis, *Swift*, vol. 3, 5.

CHAPTER SIX: Irish Hero

p. 102, "It is really a difficult matter . . ." Woolley, *Correspondence*, vol. 2, 287.

p. 103, "As the World is now . . ." Ibid., 310.

p. 107, "How grievously POOR ENGLAND . . ." Swift, *Prose Writings*, vol. 9, 18–19.

p. 107, "I SHOULD wish the parliament . . ." Ibid., 16.

p. 108, "There is so much of the Dean . . ." Woolley, *Correspondence*, vol. 2, 347.

p. 108, "Now if the Chief Justice . . ." Ibid., 345.

p. 110, "If my genius and spirit . . ." Swift, *Prose Writings*, vol. 9, 34.

p. 110, "You do not find . . ." Woolley, *Correspondence*, vol. 2, 340.

p. 110, "from the time of spilling . . ." Ibid., 343.

p. 110-111, "Shall you who have . . ." Ibid., 386.

p. 111, "I am forced to leave . . ." Ibid., 460.

p. 112, "To the Tradesmen . . ." Swift, *Prose Writings,* vol. 10, 3.

p. 113, "I do not know . . . as the Irish People." Woolley, *Correspondence*, vol. 2, 494.

p. 113, "What I intend now . . ." Swift, *Prose Writings*, vol. 10, 3.

p. 113, "THEREFORE, my Friends . . . ruin even our Beggars." Ibid., 11–12.

p. 114, "Let Mr. Wood and his . . ." Ibid., 17.

p. 114-115, "WERE not the People . . ." Ibid., 31.

p. 115, "By the Laws of GOD . . ." Ibid., 63.

p. 115, "When your Excellency shall . . ." Woolley, *Correspondence*, vol. 2, 496.

p. 116, "I could have wished . . . alter for the worse." Ibid., 498–499.

p. 116, "The principal affaire You mention . . . " Ibid., 502.

p. 116, "The work is done . . ." Woolley, *Correspondence*, vol. 2, 593.

p. 117, "That Writer is, at present . . ." Swift, *Prose Writings*, vol. 10, xxx–xxxi.

p. 117, "Mine were onely to . . ." Woolley, *Correspondence*, vol. 2, 639–640.

p. 118, "to represent the affairs . . .it would be in vain." Ibid., 642.

p. 119, "I look upon this . . ." Ibid., vol. 3, 2.

p. 119, "Your Travels I hear . . ." Ibid.,vol. 2, 597.

CHAPTER SEVEN: Gulliver

p. 121, "from the cabinet-council . . ." Woolley, *Correspondence*, vol. 2, 47.

p. 121, "I prophecy [*Gulliver's Travels*] . . ." Ibid., 52.

p. 121, "A Bishop here said . . ." Ibid., 56.

p. 121-122, "I do not remember . . ." Swift, *Gulliver's Travels* (Oxford: Oxford University Press, 2005), 7.

p. 122, "I have Reason to apprehend . . . a little dissatisfied." Ibid., 11.

p. 123, "a human Creature . . ." Ibid., 17.

p. 123, "gains Favour by his mild . . ." Ibid., 24.

p. 123, "It is allowed on all . . ." Ibid., 43.

p. 125, "only an Heap . . . the Surface of the Earth." Ibid., 120.

p. 125, "the most pernicious Race . . ." Ibid., 121.

p. 125, "had been Eight Years . . ." Ibid., 167.

p. 128, "You will wonder to find . . ." Woolley, *Correspondence*, vol. 3, 84.

p. 128, "I do not intend . . ." Ibid., 122.

p. 128, "The last Act of Life . . ." Ibid., 123.

p. 129-130, "Here I could live . . ." Swift, *Prose Writings*, vol. 5, 207.

p. 130, "My Head achs . . ." Ibid., 229.

p. 130, "She had indeed reason . . ." Ibid., 236.

p. 131, "I hear that you have . . ." Woolley, *Correspondence*, vol. 3, 157.

p. 131, "God forbid I should condemn . . ." Ibid., 180.

p. 132, "There is not one Argument . . . Effects are equally invisible." Swift, *Prose Writings*, vol. 12, 11–12.

p. 132, "I truly share in all . . ." Woolley, *Correspondence*, vol. 3, 257–258.

p. 134, "hug themselves, and reason thus . . ." Swift, *Complete Poems*, 488.

p. 135, "Poor Pope will grieve . . ." Ibid., 491.

p. 135, "Perhaps I may allow . . ." Ibid., 497.

p. 135, "He never courted men . . ." Ibid., 494.

p. 136, "an impulse foreboding . . ." Woolley, *Correspondence*, vol. 3, 563.

p. 136, "My Head is ever bad . . ." Harold Williams, *The Correspondence of Jonathan Swift* (London: Oxford University Press, 1965), vol. 4, 502.

CHAPTER EIGHT: "Swift Has Sailed into His Rest"

p. 137-138, "Your son . . . gave me . . ." Williams, *Correspondence*, vol. 5, 175.

p. 138, "I take the liberty . . ." Ibid., 188.

p. 138-139, "Wilson began to grow . . ." Ibid., 211.

p. 139-140, "He shrugged his shoulders . . . 'I am a fool'" Ibid., 214.

p. 142, "Swift has sailed into . . ." William Butler Yeats, *Collected Poems* (London: Vintage, 1992), 253.

BIBLIOGRAPHY

Arnold, Bruce. *Swift: An Illustrated Life*. Dublin: Lilliput Press, 1999.

Arnold-Baker, Charles. *The Companion to British History*. London: Routledge, 2001.

Black, Jeremy. *A History of the British Isles*. Basingstoke, UK: Palgrave Macmillan, 2003.

Connolly, S. J., ed. *The Oxford Companion to Irish History*. Oxford: Oxford University Press, 2002.

Craven, Kenneth. *Jonathan Swift and the Millennium of Madness: The Information Age in Swift's A Tale of a Tub*. Leiden, Netherlands: E. J. Brill, 1992.

Ehrenpreis, Irvin. *Swift: The Man, His Works, and the Age*. 3 vols. London: Methuen & Co., 1983.

Fox, Christopher, ed. *The Cambridge Companion to Jonathan Swift*. Cambridge: Cambridge University Press, 2003.

Glendenning, Victoria. *Jonathan Swift*. London: Hutchinson, 1998.

Heyck, Thomas William. *A History of the Peoples of the British Isles from 1688 to 1914*. London: Routledge, 2002.

Jeffares, A. Norman, ed. *Fair Liberty Was All His Cry: A Tercentenary Tribute to Jonathan Swift, 1667–1745*. London: Macmillan, 1967.

———. *Jonathan Swift*. Harhew, UK: Longman Group, 1976.

Mahony, Robert. *Jonathan Swift: The Irish Identity*. London: Yale University Press, 1995.

McMinn, Joseph. *Jonathan Swift: A Literary Life*. 3 vols. London: MacMillan Academic and Professional, 1983.

Murphy, Harold Lawson. *A History of Trinity College: Dublin from Its Foundation to 1702*. Dublin: Hodges, Figgis & Co, 1951.

Nokes, David. *Jonathan Swift: A Hypocrite Reversed*. Oxford: Oxford University Press, 1985.

Rodino, Richard H., and Hermann J. Real, eds. *Reading Swift: Papers from the Second Münster Symposium on Jonathan Swift*. Munich: Wilhelm Fink Verlag, 1993.

Ross, Ian Campbell. *Swift's Ireland*. Dublin: Eason & Son, 1983.

Rowse, A. L. *Jonathan Swift: Major Prophet*. London: Thames and Hudson, 1975.

Swift, Jonathan. *The Complete Poems*. Edited by Pat Rogers. London: Yale University Press, 1983.

———. *Gulliver's Travels*. Edited by Claude Rawson. Oxford: Oxford University Press, 2005.

———. *Journal to Stella*. Gloucester, UK: Alan Sutton Publishing Ltd, 1984.

———. *The Prose Writings of Jonathan Swift*. 14 vols. Edited by Herbert Davis. Oxford: Basil Blackwell, 1968.

Tucker, Bernard. *Jonathan Swift*. Dublin: Gill & Macmillan Ltd, 1983.

Williams, Harold, ed. *The Correspondence of Jonathan Swift*. 5 vols. London: Oxford University Press, 1965.

Williams, Kathleen, ed. *Jonathan Swift: The Critical Heritage*. London: Routledge, 1970.

Woolley, David, ed. *The Correspondence of Jonathan Swift*. 4 vols. Frankfurt: Peter Lang, 1999.

Yeats, William Butler. *Collected Poems*. Edited by Augustine Martin. London: Vintage, 1992.

WEB SITES

www.swiftsociety.com
The Kilkenny International Swift Society provides links to biographical information and Swift's complete works in prose and poetry.

www.jaffebros.com/lee/gulliver
Detailed background on *Gulliver's Travels* and supplemental information on Swift.

http://www.victorianweb.org/previctorian/swift/swiftov.html
Many articles and summaries about Swift's life, writing style, and religious beliefs. Also includes several timelines.

INDEX

Y 92 SWIFT
Aykroyd, Clarissa.
Savage satire

03-07-2007